D1730600

Us & Them

Richard Hill

A Division of Europublic SA/NV

By the same author

WeEuropeans

EuroManagers & Martians

Great Britain Little England

The NewComers: Austria, Finland and Sweden

Have You Heard This One? An Anthology of European Jokes

For the young people of Europe

With acknowledgments to a lot of people, young and old, who have given me help and encouragement, and in particular Karin, Jason and Nick.

To understand Europe, visit the Europublic site
at the following address:

URL Internet:

http://www.understanding-europe.com

Published by Europublications, Division of Europublic SA/NV,
Avenue Winston Churchill 11 (box 21), B-1180 Brussels.
Tel: + 32 2 343 77 26, Fax: + 32 2 343 93 30.

E-mail: info@europublic.com

Cover design: U&I, Brussels.

Back cover photographs: Josef Jany and Tornio Tourist Office.

Printed in Belgium. Edition et Imprimerie, Brussels.
D/1996/6421/1   ISBN 90-74440-10-X

Contents

Introduction

"Nationalist movements - linguistic, social, economic, political - are on the march, tearing apart the unitarian nation-state. In 50 years will there be a Belgium, Italy, Spain, United Kingdom as we know them today?"

Guido Brunner, ex-Member of the European Commission

"Patriotism is your conviction that your country is superior to all others because you were born in it"

George Bernard Shaw

"A state which is incompetent to satisfy different races condemns itself; a state which labours to neutralise, to absorb or to expel them is destitute of the chief basis of self-government"

Lord Acton

"A nation is a society united by a delusion about its ancestry and by a common hatred of its neighbours"

Dean William R Inge

"Democracy was born with the sense of nationality. The two are inherently linked, and neither can be fully understood apart from this connection"

Liah Greenfield, *'Nationalism: Five Roads to Modernity'*

"We may suggest that a nation is in effect any assembly, mixture, or confusion of people which is either afflicted by or wishes to be afflicted by a foreign office of its own, in order to behave collectively as if its needs, desires, and vanities were beyond comparison more important than the general welfare of humanity"

H G Wells, *'The Outline of History'*

"When you rave, no one cares about nationalities"

Gibraltarian disco dancer

To discern the real difference between one European country and another, cross the frontier on the ground by car, train or even better on foot. From the air, you may see the physical differences - the geography, the crops, the way the fields are tilled - but you will not have the sense of shock that the sights and smells of land-based travel afford. On top of which, one airport looks very much like another.

Frontiers have been and still are the charm and, at the same time, the challenge of Europe. We tend to be fascinated by them: they conjure up visions of mystery, strange ways, new experiences. Sometimes they convey a sense of menace, at other times a hint of romance, but always anticipation of one kind or another.

Some frontiers make evident sense geographically. Mountains, rivers, seas have determined the outlines of many of the European states. In some cases even weather patterns seem to play a part.

But most frontiers have been shaped by the states themselves, through acts of aggression, infiltration or dynastic marriages. As old 'front lines', practically or psychologically, they now betray their past in subtle ways. There are differences in road surfaces, changes in the way the fields are patterned and partitioned.

Sometimes these fields are open, betraying their historical role in providing a clear line of fire against attacking forces. Forests, in contrast, have been left thick with undergrowth to provide a natural defence. Less subtle signs are abandoned fortifications, even watchtowers.

These are Europe's 'no-man's-lands'. Until the Single Market and Maastricht work their magic, they will remain transit zones, with local people crossing regularly to work or to shop. Some of them have survived, fortuitously, as nature reserves. Others make their presence felt when your mobile phone refuses to work.

11

But most frontiers make little sense today from any point of view. Some of them cut cultures in two. Others - and this applies to a lot of them - encapsulate cultures that are non-homogeneous or even incompatible. They are places of contradiction, of overcharged history, of people who have in some cases changed nationality six or seven times.

In fact, our frontiers have never made any real sense racially or genetically. Science has shown that cases of so-called 'racial purity' can be counted on the fingers of one hand. Over two millenia Europe has seen too many movements and too much miscegenation of peoples for it to be otherwise.

In today's world, our frontiers also make little sense politically. Despite the sentimental attachment of many of its people, the nation-state is losing its relevance in a number of respects. And, if the opinion of the younger generations of Europeans set out in chapter 8 has any meaning, it is in danger of losing its legitimacy as well.

The nation-state was and is a circumstantial artefact of individual ambition, dynastic marriages, trade policies, mass aggression and, in the case of the younger European states, macro-muddle (see box, pages 14-15).

While it has almost outlived its usefulness politically it remains, culturally, a reality of sorts, though often a very imperfect one. When you cross a frontier, even if there are no physical barriers - mountains, rivers, seas or customs posts, where these still exist - you are aware that you have entered another world, whether you judge this from the way the roads are paved, the houses are built, or the fields are tended.

In subtler ways, the people are different too - and not just because, as is so often the case in Europe, they happen to speak another language than your own. Cultures shape behaviour patterns and, even more subtly and significantly, ways of reasoning and value systems as well.

The result is what we tend to call 'national character', something that is reflected shorthand-style in the minds of others - and often in the minds of the people themselves - as stereotypes.

Stereotypes are inevitably suspect. Yet they are often the product of accumulated folk wisdom and they often contain a grain of wisdom. As far back as 1632 an English traveller, William Lithgow, recorded a Sicilian proverb: "The French are wiser than they seem, and the Spanish seem wiser than they are". This still has the ring of truth today.

So Europeans differ. But we surely have one thing in common: wherever you happen to be at the time, sooner or later you are likely to do or say something that triggers the 'Not Invented Here' response. Its most frequent expression is the comment "that's the way we've always done things" or, more finitely, "that's impossible"!

Behind the response lies the 'Us & Them' syndrome. I've had this reaction in every European country I have visited, even Malta - which, being a very small country by European standards and an island at that, is perhaps understandable.

The reaction is prompted largely by certain perceived differences, whether in appearance, in behaviour, in ways of reasoning, in sense of humour, or in value judgements. However much the European Union may harmonise the technical and practical things in life - and the EU has made impressive progress in the last ten years - these cultural differences will remain, thank God, and with justification. They are the spice of Europe.

These so-called 'national cultures' will certainly survive, despite the onslaught of the mass media and global commercialism. Programmed into the minds of people they are indeed a reality of sorts, but often a politically inspired and artificially inflated reality and one that the elite of most European nations is only too happy to reinforce.

13

Europe à la carte

"May 13, Tuesday [1919] - Go round to the Rue Nitot. We first go up to A.J.B.'s flat and then down to Lloyd George's flat. Barnes, the Labour minister attached to our delegation, is there. He is interested in the Adriatic for some odd reason. We then move into the dining room. I spread out my big map on the dinner table and they all gather round.

We are still discussing when the flabby Orlando and the sturdy Sonnino are shown into the dining room. They all sit round the map. The appearance of a pie about to distributed is thus enhanced. Ll.G shows them what he suggests. They ask for Scala Nova as well. 'Oh,no!' says Ll.G. 'You can't have that - it's full of Greeks!' He goes on to point out that there are further Greeks at Makri, and a whole wedge of them along the coast toward Alexandretta. 'Oh, no,' I whisper to him, 'there are not many Greeks there'.

'But yes,' he answers, 'don't you see it's coloured green?' I then realise that he mistakes my map for an ethnological map, and thinks the green means Greeks instead of valleys, and the brown means Turks instead of mountains. Ll.G takes this correction with great good humour. He is as quick as a kingfisher. Meanwhile Orlando and Sonnino chatter to themselves in Italian. Finally thay appear ready to accept a mandate over the Adalia region, but it is not clear whether in return they will abandon Fiume and Rhodes.

We get out the League Covenant regarding Mandates. We observe that this article provides for 'the consent and wishes of the people concerned'. They find that phrase very amusing. Orlando's white cheeks wobble with laughter and his puffy eyes fill with tears of mirth.

We agree to put it all down on paper. I leave with Balfour...

... The door opens. A heavily furnished study with my huge map on the carpet. Bending over it (bubble, bubble, toil and trouble) are Clemenceau, Ll.G and P.W. They have pulled up armchairs and crouch low over the map. Ll.G. says - genial always - 'Now, Nicolson, listen with all your ears.' He then proceeds to expound the agreement which they have reached. I make certain minor suggestions. I also point out that they are cutting the Baghdad Railway. This is brushed aside. P.W. says, 'And what about the islands?'

'They are', I answer firmly, 'Greek islands, Mr. President.'
'Then they should go to Greece?'
H.N.: 'Rather!'
P.W.: 'Rather!'

Anyhow I am told to go off and draft resolutions at once. Clemenceau says nothing during all of this. He sits at the edge of his chair and leans his two blue-gloved hands down upon the map. More than ever does he look like a gorilla of yellow ivory.

I dash back to the Astoria and dictate resolutions. They work out as follows: (1) Turkey to be driven out of Europe and Armenia. (2) Greece to have the Smyrna-Aivali Zone and a mandate over most of the Vilayet of Aidin. (3) Italy to get a mandate over South Asia Minor from Marmarice to Mersina, plus Konia. (4) France to get the rest.

It is immoral and impracticable. But I obey my orders. The Greeks are getting too much."
Harold Nicolson, 'Peacemaking 1919'

A.J.B. = A. J. Balfour, British Foreign Minister; Ll.G. = David Lloyd George, British Prime Minister; Orlando = Vittorio Orlando, Italian Prime Minister; Sonnino = Giorgio Sonnino, Italian Foreign Minister; P.W. = Woodrow Wilson, US President; Clemenceau = Georges Clemenceau, French Prime Minister; League = League of Nations.

What a way to run the world! At least we've learned something since - or have we (Bosnia-Herzegovina)?

Like the nation-states themselves, Europe's national cultures often reflect an act of political will that was relevant to the time and circumstances but not to the issues that face us today.

These national cultures and their consequences - the 'dotted lines' inside the minds of men and women - are the only real frontiers left. They are still the most distinctive and durable feature of Europe, yet they could also be its nemesis. The evidence of recent events in eastern Europe is enough to prove the point.

A seething mass of sub-cultures

Within these national cultures, myriad subcultures are embedded, regional, community, linguistic, religious and others. These add to, and quite often subtract from, the whole. The spirit of localism is still very much alive in countries as dissimilar as Greece, Belgium and Finland. Forgetting the folklore, regional cultures are just as evident in the larger nations of Britain, Germany and France.

In reality, it would be wrong to think that the European nations and their peoples have always seemed as distinctive as they are today. It was only with the advent of modern European nationalism, as described in the next chapter, that politically inspired exploitation of these differences became commonplace.

Moreover 'national character' was, over the years, subject to some pretty radical transformations. People changed in terms of both values and habits. Until the Italians arrived at the court of Henri II with Catherine de Medici, the French never gesticulated, ate decent food or used perfume. The British picked the queueing habit up from the French. And, not all that long ago the Germans, according to their contemporaries, were a wild, undisciplined lot and lousy soldiers.

Indeed, many of the things that make one country different from another are of relatively recent origin. The tulip - now symbolically, even stereotypically Dutch - was introduced from Turkey to Holland in the late-16th century. The plane trees that line, elegantly but dangerously, the *routes nationales* of France so beloved of foreigners in the pre-motorway age, only arrived in Europe from Iran in the 18th century. And the moors of Scotland and the bogs of Ireland belie countries that used to be forested from coast to coast.

So, inevitably, it goes with political fashions too. Dispel the hype and you find that many of our countries only emerged as sovereign nation-states in the course of the last two centuries. The patina of authority and uniformity they have acquired lies thinly over the underlying reality of this seething mass of sub-cultures, regional and social.

Look at the map of Europe as it has evolved over the last thousand years and you will see that the frontiers have shifted constantly like the images in a kaleidoscope. Yet, with the rise of nationalism in its various forms over the last two centuries, we have come to see these divisions as real and immutable.

In fact, never since the *Völkerwanderungen* - the great migrations of the first millenium when dotted lines didn't count in any case - have so many people moved across the frontiers of Europe's nation-states as during and since World War Two. Yet with the exception of the ex-communist world of central and eastern Europe national boundaries, with all their arbitrariness and injustices, have stayed virtually unchanged this last half-century.

In the words of Per Magnus Wijkman, "to be European is to belong to a community of foreigners". As people who, one thousand years ago, knew little of frontiers and were often genetically related in a myriad of liaisons, reflecting our migrant histories, we as Europeans should marvel at the identities we have created for our countries and for ourselves in the meantime.

Seeded as states of mind - the human will to bond with those one feels closest to - they have burgeoned into nation-states, with all their panoply and sentiment. They have co-alesced in perceived differences that have, at best, encouraged the 'Us & Them' syndrome intrinsic in human nature and, at worst, led to the bloodiest of wars.

There are of course many real differences - Europe would be a dull place if that were not the case - but they are by no means exclusive to the nation-state. And the arrogation of such differences by this relatively recent and man-made system, reinforced by sentiments of cultural superiority and sovereignty, lies at the heart of many of the problems we face today.

Yet the signs of a sea-change are there. In Europe, we live with the irony that we are instinctively developing strong-er regional identities at the same time as we are more cogni-tively working towards a United Europe. Where this leaves the nation-state, the pig in the middle, remains to be seen.

At all events there are compelling reasons to open up the debate. The political disaffection of European youth described in chapter 8 of this book is one of them.

Apart from the questionable morality of any form of sep-aratism - which is ultimately what nationalism amounts to - our atavistic attachment to nationhood and sovereignty is challenged as never before by the globalisation of our lives. Whether this is a good thing or a bad thing is hardly the point. The fact is that what was fine for the 19th century is almost by definition no longer right for the 21st.

Even if it is a bit of a misnomer to talk about 'nationalist movements', Guido Brunner sets us off by posing the right question. Will there be a Belgium, Italy, Spain, United Kingdom in 50 years time, not to mention all the others?

Moreover, does this ultimately matter? As Jean-Baptiste Duroselle says in his book 'Europe: A History of its Peoples': "Nationalism, and the fragmentation of Europe into nation-states, are relatively recent phenomena: they may be temporary, and are certainly not irreversible".

The nation-state has seen us through thick and thin over the last 200 years, some of them pretty unhappy ones at that. Might it not be time for something new? That is what this book is about.

There is a growing community of people who find the concepts of nationhood and sovereignty strangely old-fashioned. I happen to be one of them.

Through accidents of birth, expatriate childhood, the environment of mixed marriages or, as in my case, the vicissitudes of life, we have the unparalleled opportunity to acquire a distance, even a release, from our national ties.

This does not make our affection for our nationality and native culture any the less real. It's just that we find solace and inspiration in other cultures as well. They all have their good sides and bad sides. The only difference between them is that they are, well, different. But there's always a reason why and, once you understand the reason, these cultures become as familiar and friendly as your own.

Once you achieve that state of bliss, aggressive and mindless attachment to your mother-country and mother-culture is out of the question. While you humanly and inevitably retain much of your original culture, you realise that where you happen to have been born is irrelevant to the greater order of things.

I hope it was nothing more than a Freudian slip that caused an eminent British business school to talk about 'ex-patriot managers', a class to which I belong...

The Search
for an Identity

"But why identify ourselves with a country - such an artificial, unnatural and recent creation? Why not with our family? Or village? Or town? Or political party? Or class? Or continent? Or planet?"

George Mikes, Hungarian author

"In times of social and cultural confusion or uncertainty, as presently in Europe, in the United States, and in other parts of the world, people seem to feel a psychological need for stability and order... an unconscious search for profiling, demarcating, group orientation, historical heritage"

Professor Åke Daun, Stockholm University

"No government, unless it is prepared to rely entirely on brute force, can do its job properly in the modern world if the people it governs do not have a clear-cut sense of identity that they share with the government - unless, in other words, they are both part of the 'we'"

'The Economist', 5/1/1996

"There is no intrinsic difference between the national pride of Norway and that of Serbia, except that it is expressed in different ways"   **Sir Peter Ustinov, *'The European'***

"There is no more effective way of bonding together the disparate sections of restless peoples than to unite them against outsiders"

Eric Hobsbawm, *'Nations and Nationalism Since 1780'*

"Names and national symbols of countries are not unimportant. They play a significant part in defining identity and it is patronising to suggest that they constitute 'nonsense' or 'absurdity'. Usurping them, and turning them into vehicles for historical falsifications and territorial claims against neighbours, can bring friction, conflict and instability"

Dr Filippos S Mavroskoufis, vice-chairman of the
Macedonian Society of Great Britain, in a letter to *'The European'*

George Mikes posed the questions opposite in a magazine article twenty years ago. His options now look rather out-of-date.

Family, OK, particularly if you happen to be Italian or from one of the collectivist cultures. Village, that's pushing it a bit. Town, maybe. Political party, definitely not, if you listen to the younger generations in Europe. Class, too subjective a category, varying from one European country to another: some are almost classless, unless you count 'class' as how much money you have or make. Continent, OK, why not Europe? Planet, sure, but still perhaps a bit premature.

But what about region, something that George Mikes omitted to mention? Look at what's happened in the twenty years since he wrote these words. Something is rustling these days in the national undergrowth: people's roots. At the same time as trying to resolve our international differences by creating wider alliances - led by the European Union in our part of the world - we are identifying increasingly with our local or regional cultures.

Although best remembered as a humourist, George Mikes had some important things to say about identity - after all, as one of central Europe's many 20th-century emigrés, he successfully made the transition from the Hungarian to the British culture - no mean achievement at any time! He spoke from experience.

In the same article, Mikes said: "It was the cool, selfish interest of individuals that made them form large families, tribes and states and it was only later that the State invested itself with mythical attributes and demanded a life-and-death loyalty."

Though a highly condensed and rather cavalier assessment of the origins of the nation-state, George Mikes' words encapsulate the essence of the phenomenon.

23

If we draw up a balance sheet of the European nation-state today, how do things look? On the assets side, it has provided us with the institutions and disciplines necessary to ensure the 'social contract' essential to progress and prosperity. The latter has been unevenly shared, yet the benefits to the majority are irrefutable.

The nation-state has made us its children. It has succoured and educated us. It has shielded us from our common enemies.

On the liabilities side, however, it has made us acutely aware of the differences between 'Us' and 'Them' when, in many cases, there are no great differences - certainly not ones that, at the human level, are irreconcilable.

In so doing, it has taught us to fight and kill, shedding the blood of "Them" with a lust and enthusiasm that we would not accord to the slaughter of animals. It has sent us on crusades and colonial adventures which have, at their best, been thoughtless and, at worst, brutal. And it has done wonders in mythmaking and reinventing our pasts.

It is impossible to say whether the net results shown on this balance sheet are positive or negative: we are comparing things that cannot be compared. But, if you add some of the more recent liabilities of the nation-state - its squandering of precious resources on high-profile projects and 'throw-away' arms when so many people are out of work, its marginalisation of sections of society and, most seriously, alarming deviations from normal democratic standards - then the balance looks less than positive.

The bonding instinct

Folk need something to relate to. Driven by a fundamental urge to find identity in a group, if the grounds for such an identity are not forthcoming, they will invent them.

Europe is no exception. In the words of the past rector of the College of Europe, Hendrik Brugmans, "the profound need for roots seems to have been given by nature itself to Europe".

The people of central and eastern Europe, recently and abruptly deprived of the attentions of an authoritarian nanny-state, found reassurance in a variety of pursuits ranging from religion, including the strangest of cults, to rank nationalism and irredentism.

The bonding instinct is highly developed in the human being: people need to belong. We are all, most of us anyway, in search of an identity we can share with our fellow-beings to help us feel more secure. Those of us who aren't tend to be treated as eccentrics, masochists, recluses or outcasts.

By the same token, human beings hate ambiguity, and fear of ambiguity can breed ethnocentrism - I would rather say 'culturocentrism' - and by extension racism.

My own assessment of the *physical* expression of the identity phenomenon takes in a longer series of steps than George Mikes': family, then tribe (both with the help of language); mutual interest groups, in particular the lord-vassal relationship of feudal Europe; community/city; region; country; nation-state. To these I would add all the c-words - clans, clubs, circles, cliques, castes, classes, coteries, caucases, cabals, camorras, conclaves, committees, etc - and of course the big M-word.

The *intellectual* expression of a common identity, historically a cult, religion or cause, is also a powerful bonding agent that can reinforce the geographical/physical relationship or, as in the case of Buddhism, ignore it entirely.

Other intellectual identities have burgeoned in the last two hundred years: first with the political emanations culminating in the manicheistic standoff between capitalism and communism; secondly with the idealistic ones typified by environmentalism, consumerism, animal rights, and the like.

Increasingly, we are witnessing a fragmentation of society into in-groups, to the extent that today's youth prefers to identify with a subculture - Technos, Rappers, Hillbillies, Punks, etc - rather than with general cultures. Recent evidence also suggests that young Europeans are more interested in associating over a single issue than in clubbing together in the social sense.

T-shorts, stickers, pinboards and the like

There are, of course, many tangible ways of creating or reinforcing a sense of identity. One of the most popular traditionally has been the use of 'icons', the symbolism of flags, insignia, national anthems and the like. Only recently, big fights erupted in central and eastern Europe as the ex-communist countries made competitive claims to colours, symbols, tunes and ditties as part of the process of reestablishing their national identities.

Another technique, effective at both the social and the personal levels, is the wearing of uniforms - something that is viewed by the intelligentsia as a refuge for the feeble-minded, but which can be very attractive even to the educated. Medals, much appreciated by *anciens combattants* from France to Finland, can add the finishing touch.

Happily, today, uniforms and medals are giving way to T-shirts, stickers, pinboards and the like. But other types of 'uniform' - yuppie pinstripes, baggy trousers, clumpy hi-tech sneaker boots, jeans and check shirts, depending on the age group - testify to the undiminished power of the bonding instinct.

The search for symbols also contributes to society's attachment to things like national airlines, automobile and aircraft manufacturers, defence industries and shipbuilders.

Nationhood, if not nationalism, distorts the business map of Europe. National concerns like airlines and arms manufacturers - both a great inspiration of national pride - benefit from hidden or overt protectionism.

As the chairman of the Fokker aviation group said at the time of his company's bankruptcy: "The collapse of this industry is very damaging for the standing of the Netherlands in the world". Now even Albania has its own national stock exchange. Swissair on the other hand - the Swiss being practically minded and profit-oriented people - has transferred its accounts department to India.

Even pan-European ventures like Airbus and the ill-fated Eurodata computer consortium are victims of political carve-ups. Amadeus, the airline reservation system, is jointly owned by Iberia, Air France and Lufthansa, in association with Continental Airlines of the US. The result is that it has its corporate HQ in Madrid, its development and marketing operations in Sophia Antipolis near Nice, and its mainframe computers in Munich. Such a setup - echoing the political geography forced by the nation-states on the European Union's own institutions - is certainly not the one an efficiency expert would recommend...

National self-interest is also very much in evidence in areas like insurance, intellectual property, recognition of qualifications, and public procurement. The alibi of sovereignty is a breeding ground for proprietary impulses to protect or promote 'one's own', whether one's own is under threat or not.

"We won the second half"

Not all that long ago the most potent expression and endorsement of the national bonding instinct was war.

To quote from Paul Kennedy's book 'The Rise and Fall of the Great Powers': "Military factors - or better, geostrategical factors - helped to shape the territorial boundaries of these new nation-states, while the frequent wars induced national consciousness, in a negative fashion at least, in that Englishmen learned to hate Spaniards, Swedes to hate Danes, Dutch rebels to hate their former Habsburg overlords."

Today, the single most potent expression of identity common to all of Europe and, for that matter, most of the rest of the world is the football club. "Nothing unleashes passions and hooligan instincts as wildly as football", said George Mikes. "Nothing gives you the feeling of *belonging*, nothing gives you a stronger identity than supporting the same team."

Even that great authority on nationalism, the Vienna-born historian Eric Hobsbawm, recognised the rallying potential of the game. Speaking of his childhood in the 1920s he said: "The only thing that brought the Austrians together in those days was football". More recently a UK journalist described football as "a sport which, more than any other institution, religion, culture or creed embraces every class of people" (I'm not so sure about the English upper classes!).

Today, the European Championships burnish and quite often tarnish the emblems of the nation-states - to the extent that the Norwegian press runs headlines like "We won the second half", when reporting a 2-1 defeat by Sweden, and "We beat England 1-1", when commenting on a draw.

But, then, the Norwegians are well-known for their boisterous nationalism, the kind that prompted Aase Kleveland, a government minister, to declare that the other European nation-states were run by "barbarians out to destroy Norwegian culture"!

Barbarians is a description most frequently attributed to football fans, with some reason. According to Dougie and Eddy Brimson, self-styled experts on the British hooligan's mind (he does have one), "people fight because people like to fight. Soccer is the vehicle they use because they can justify violence as the defence of their team, town or reputation. They see their role as an extension of that of their teams: to beat the opposition. Violence is like smoking. If you try it once and hate it, you don't do it again. But if you like it, it's bloody hard to give it up."

International football is a fine substitute for war but the language is familiar. Commenting a defeat of Germany by Russia in an international match, a football coach described it as a "revenge for Stalingrad". In the run-up to the match with Spain in the Euro 96 championships, British media evoked memories of the defeat of the Armada, the Spanish Inquisition and even the Spanish flu'. When England confronted the Germans in the semi-finals, the talk was of the Blitz, Spitfires and the like. Periodical aggression, maybe, but it's better than all-out war.

The sense of identity is equally strong, if not stronger, at the level of the local team. The fact that the team carries the name of the town - even when most of the players are strangers or outright foreigners - is enough to ensure the strongest possible sense of identity, the geographically linked kind.

By the same token not just football, but any international event pitting the sporting heroes of one country against those of another - an international athletics meetings, a tennis tournament, ice skating, Formula One racing - is guaranteed to foster the national bonding instinct. Moreover, in the words of 'The Economist', "sporting success somehow confers political legitimacy".

The spirit of cultural rivalry, both friendly and unfriendly, is also present in microcosm: Punks, Technos, Rappers, etc. One example is the 'Hell's Angels' of Malmö, Sweden, who regularly take the ferry and their Harley-Davidsons to Copenhagen to beat up the local Harley-Davidson opposition...

The process is accelerated by national TV networks which focus on the achievements of their heroes to the detriment of others, as was so evident at the Atlanta Olympics. But football retains the distinction of being the one sport where the audience most often joins in physically as well...

My grandmother wants her bike back!

In today's western Europe, a number of the smaller countries - the Netherlands, Denmark and Norway in particular - do a good job of feeling proud of their identities. They are entitled to make the most of what they have.

Yet even a sensible people like the Dutch - who, despite their cheekily impressive maritime and mercantile past, have earned a reputation as a relatively fair and open-minded people - manage to draw from time to time on hidden wells of prejudice. Their favourite sport is being beastly to the Germans: there are still little old Dutch ladies who refuse to serve German tourists because they are German.

Only recently, the rather undignified abandonment by Daimler-Benz of its investment in the ailing Fokker aircraft company prompted Dutch economics minister Hans Wijers to warn against any resurgence of anti-German feeling, still there below the surface. Of course aircraft and defence companies, state airlines and nuclear weapons - all in various degrees macho expressions of human activity - are guaranteed to promote feelings of national pride.

But the most extraordinary thing is that even Dutch youth - people two generations removed from the Second World War and all that went with it - also live with this hangover. In their case the great catalyst was the European Football Championships (here we go again!) where they resorted to open warfare. The only light relief, if that's the right phrase, was provided by the placards borne by Dutch supporters with the legend: "My grandmother wants her bike back!". This was again a reference to WWII...

The only western European country that seems to have largely escaped the virus of nationalism, though it has every reason to be proud of its history and its culture, is Sweden. Professor Daun, the country's leading sociologist, comments that "Sweden's national day, June 6, has never been experienced by Swedes as a day of special joy or public celebration" (unlike the national day, May 17, of Sweden's Norwegian neighbours, who are highly nationalistic by comparison).

When asked "How proud are you to be Swedish?", only 28 per cent of Swedes said "very proud". By comparison, when Americans were asked the same question about their allegiance to the United States, 80 per cent of them said "very proud".

While human foibles make the need for an identity a subconscious and inescapable process, there have been many conscious efforts in recent European history to reinforce these identities. As often as not, the arguments used have been factious and ill-informed, in some cases pure mythmaking. Belief in ethnic superiority, buttressed by claims of ethnic purity, is the biggest spoof of all.

Hitler Germany's evocation of the Nordic and so-called Aryan *Supermensch* is only one example, albeit the worst. The Victorian British perverted the record of the Icelandic 'Vikings' in order to justify their own apparent prowess in matters of trade and domination. The Greeks, with the help of the British, fabricated the Hellenic ideal. And so on.

When nationalism gets out of hand, it opens a Pandora's box of consequences - in some cases war, in others the emergence of nationalist movements in neighbouring communities and maybe war as a result. A perfect example of this 'nationalism in opposition' is the effect of the still relatively young state of Israel in catalysing a parallel movement focussed on an area, Palestine, which previously had no clear identity among Arabs.

Another expression of the 'Us & Them' syndrome is our different national interpretations of our common European history. One of the gaps in the knowledge of many of Britain's schoolchildren is the truth of the country's conduct in the Boer War. Yet Italian schoolchildren were taught, until not long ago, that the Boer War was the most despicable event in European colonial history - and the Italian escapade in Abyssinia its finest!

French students until recently learned little about facts and events outside *La Patrie*, to the extent that one university graduate I met was incapable of placing the Netherlands on the map of Europe and another, who indeed knew where the country was, asked what the skiing was like there!

Happily, books are now emerging which present European history in a less ethnocentric (culturocentric) way, largely and perhaps surprisingly due to the initiative of some French historians.

Community spirit, common interest, cooperation

Another and more constructive version of the bonding instinct based on geographical proximity is increasingly evident at the level of local and regional business and industry. Some towns and regions of Europe have succeeded in fostering a community spirit, a sense of common interest and a tradition of cooperation which gives them a natural advantage in manufacturing and trade.

The SME sector of industry - as characterised by the economies of Austria, Catalonia and many of the cities of northern Italy - has shown itself to be resistant to reductions in employment levels during economic slowdowns.

The identification of small and medium enterprises (SMEs) with their local communities, with the boss knowing his workers as neighbours and supporters of the same football team (here we go again!), produces an apparent reluctance to fire people when the going is tough.

In the recession of the mid-90s Austria, which has few big industries, recorded an overall unemployment rate of only 5 per cent - as did Biella, a typical example of the northern Italian phenomenon of a community essentially dedicated to a single industry and vertically integrated as a result. Even the Barcelona region, which has a lot of ailing industries, still came significantly below the European average with 9 per cent unemployment.

Another example of this phenomenon is the German state of Baden-Württemberg which, with a few big employers like Bosch and Mercedes-Benz surrounded by a huge community of SME subcontractors, has a jobless rate at the time of writing of only 7.2 per cent.

Curiously, the state owes the existence of its *Mittelstand*, as German SMEs are called, largely to the fact that it operates an egalitarian inheritance system untypical of most German states, which apply the law of primogeniture.

The result is that children inherit a tidy sum of money but not enough to live off. So, with the help of a solid apprenticeship at which German society excels, they set out on life by starting up a small business, as likely as not a machine shop or something similar.

Unrelated evidence of the power of localism is provided by the dramatic growth throughout Europe, with the help of new technologies, of media that identify with the local communities they serve. That a country like Spain should have independent TV stations transmitting to separate small communities no more than 20 kilometres apart would have been unthinkable a decade ago.

Television producers in most European countries have reported a subtle shift in viewer priorities since the early-90s, partly no doubt reflecting the troubled times we live in, but also pointing to something deeper. They detect a trend in demand away from international news and documentaries towards domestic issues: national or even regional news. This applies as much to the United Kingdom as it does to Austria and Finland.

Regardless of the composition - listeners to local radio/TV, football fans or citizens of a nation-state - any in-group is likely to be associated with somewhere on the map. As the French say, "*ici, je suis chez moi*". Everyone feels at home, somewhere or other.

Real Estate, Nation-State

"Whenever people have different answers to the questions 'What is your land?' and 'Who are your people?' there is room for division"

'The Economist', 23/9/1995

"Come the day when 80 per cent of the population of the Dordogne will be English, then it will not quite be the Dordogne even if the English there are very amiable"

Jean-Yves Le Gallou, French right-wing politician

"We know too little about what went on, or for that matter what still goes on, in the minds of most relatively inarticulate men and women, to speak with any confidence about their thoughts and feelings towards the nationalities and nation-states which claim their loyalties"

E J Hobsbawm, *'Nations and Nationalism Since 1780'*

"Particular attention should be paid [to] the sensitivity of the Greeks towards the historical continuity of their race since antiquity through medieval Byzantium down to the present"

'Macedonia, History and Politics', Society for Macedonian Studies, Athens

"A child asks, 'Grandfather, you've been to Hungary, Ukraine, Russia and now Slovakia. How did you do it?'. The grandfather answers: 'I never left the village'."

Slovak Hungarian joke

"Nations as a natural, God-given way of classifying men, as an inherent... political destiny, are a myth; nationalism, which sometimes takes pre-existing cultures and turns them into nations, sometimes invents them, and often obliterates pre-existing cultures: that is a reality"

Ernest Gellner, 'Nations and Nationalism'

"Getting its history wrong is part of being a nation"

Ernest Renan

In most cases there is a link between identity and, in some form or another, land: a location, a vaguely defined region, or a clearly specified piece of real estate like the grounds of the local football club.

Land acquisition was a powerful motive, though by no means the only one, for the expansionist period of feudal Europe in the Early Middle Ages, before the nation-state in its modern sense emerged. More often than not, the new aristocracy took its surname from the descriptive name of the lands it acquired. Names, as Robert Bartlett states in his book 'The Making of Europe', are "tokens of identity".

Not just for the aristocracy. A study of European names is an object-lesson in the different cultural interpretations of identity. Some Spanish and many Nordic and old English surnames, like my own, are based on topographical features: we have Swedish neighbours who delight in the name of Granqvist which means 'twig of the firtree'. Maria Theresia gave descriptive names like rosetree and willowtree to many of her Jewish subjects in the Austro-Hungarian Empire.

Other cultures worked from the first name. Spanish catholics modified their first names to provide surnames for adopted Muslim converts (e.g. Gonzalo=Gonzalez, Alvaro= Alvarez). And then, in other languages, many names derived directly from the first names of the father (e.g. Petersen, Andersson, Johnson, Christopoulos, Ivanovitch, etc).

In Iceland, a first-name and sensibly feminist society, the girls acquire their own incontrovertible identity: a son whose father is called Helge will be named Helgason, but the daughter is Helgadottir. Even Spain carries historic identities forward as in the name of Hidalgo (= *hijo de algo* = son of somebody), which is more complimentary than it may sound.

The ultimate geographical identity - and without question the most powerful factor of all in the search for identity

- is the claim to exclusive rights to a part of God's Earth. Paraphrasing Crocodile Dundee, it's like two fleas arguing over who owns the dog they're on.

At the level of the individual, land ownership is a necessary ingredient of social order, the one significant exception in Europe being the Gypsies, God bless them. The Sami - who always considered their reindeer pastures 'their own', maybe because nobody else wanted them - have now started to settle and become formal landowners.

Yet, as the Nordics have shown with their 'Everyman's Law' which guarantees public right of access to the countryside, ownership should not deprive people of the enjoyment of their common heritage, as is the case in so many other European countries.

There ought to be a world of difference between feeling at home somewhere and wanting to own the place. At the level of a community, claim to exclusive ownership of an area of the globe, a concept legalised with the emergence of the nation-state, can be the first step down the road to racism.

It is noticeable that the most violent forms of fundamentalism, political or religious, tend to pivot on property. Look at the Orthodox Jewish communities on the West Bank of the Jordan, consider the land ownership claims that contributed to the breakup of Yugoslavia.

Identification with a slice of God's Earth has been the catalyst of much that is worst in recent European history. As the authors of 'The Origins of European Identity' point out, "the belief in the mystique of a soil on which a 'national spirit' would develop was a romantic notion which was to prove so harmful to Europe, particularly since it was undefinable and irrational and was radically opposed to the idea of rights attaching to man and not to a territory."

Not long ago, the republic of Georgia attempted to claim back land from one of its neighbours on the strength of a 14th-century map! As Robert Kaplan says in his book 'Balkan Ghosts': "Each nation demands that its borders revert to where they were at the exact time when its own empire had reached its zenith of ancient medieval expansion." But six-centuries-old historical evidence may still be worth more than territorial claims - of which there are many - that owe their origins to oft forgotten acts of aggression in more recent times.

On the other hand, the proprietary attitudes of farming folk who tend the land is an understandable one. In the 18th century, Catherine the Great invited German peasants to settle in the Volga region where they have lived ever since, apart from a period of banishment under Stalin to Kazakhstan (the population of the Soviet Union at the time of its break-up included well over one million Volga Germans, an additional one million ethnic Germans and one million Pontic Greeks). The Volga Germans, in particular, earned a reputation for their discipline, hard work, and respect for their German heritage.

When asked by a German TV reporter why he wanted to stay in Russia, an elderly Volga German farmer said, quite simply, *das Land gehört uns* ("the land belongs to us"), reflecting his belief that, while the Russians were happier drinking vodka than planting trees, his own people had invested their lives in the soil.

The property of Palaeolithic Man

For most of us, our link with the land is less visceral but often just as pronounced. Yet anthropologists say that some of the most contented people in this world are nomads, for example the people of North Africa, both east and west. They feel no compunction to commit themselves to a piece of real estate - and are all the happier, if not the better, for it.

Even today land claims, encouraged by speculation on what lies underneath, can lead to tragi-comic confrontations like a recent one between Greeks and Turks, battling with their national flags on a couple of goat-infested rocky islets in the eastern Aegean.

The voluntary cession of a piece of land by one sovereign state to another is a rare occurrence, if only because national pride gets in the way. When it happens to be a few hundred square meters of research base in the Antarctic - the subject of a recent deal between Britain and Ukraine - nobody minds.

It might be salutary to remind ourselves from time to time that Aquitaine once belonged to England, that the Val d'Aosta was once part of France, and that Skåne in southern Sweden was once a province of Denmark. Needless to say, the whole of Europe was once the property of Palaeolithic Man before the Celts came along - followed by the Vandals, the Goths and God knows who else.

Today, the inclination to anchor one's identity in a piece of geography is as strong as at any time in European history. In the words of Belgian sociologist Anne Morelli: "The end of nationalist Belgium might have been the end of unitarist myths and opened an era where history schoolbooks would have been made of nuances, interrogations and plural approaches. This expectation has not been met because Belgian nationalism has been immediately replaced by new territory-based identities, either regional or European." Here we go again...

Today's leisure society has also generated another dimension to the land issue. Sweden, Finland, Denmark and now Austria have all introduced legislation - in the case of Denmark, written into the Maastricht Treaty - to restrict or even bar the purchase of land or property by foreigners for holiday residences. For foreigners, read 'Germans' who, first of all, have the money to indulge themselves and, secondly, welcome any excuse to get away from the mother-country whenever they can.

Life, in short, tends to be monopolised by three kinds of people: people who live for possessions, people who live for ideas, and people who aren't interested in anything in particular. There are quite a lot in the last category. Depending on your outlook, they could be classed as at worst wasteful, at best harmless.

But most people are interested in something - and, of the first two categories, it is the people interested in possessions who are in the majority.

This simple reality lies at the heart of the human dilemma. We want to learn to live in harmony, but the values we hold often make this difficult. The human social experiment, despite the collapse of communism and the smugness of western commentators, is still in its formative years.

An article in 'The Economist' of January 5 1996 ('The nation-state is dead. Long live the nation-state') said, among other things, the following: "... communism's fall does not mean that ideology has ceased to exist. What demolished the communist idea was the superior strength of a rival body of ideas, free-market democracy, which was powerful enough to hold together the 16 countries of the West's alliance through all the alarms and rigours of the cold war."

Communism failed not because the system benefited an elite *nomenklatura* - capitalism does the same - but because it failed to take into account the independently minded and entrepreneurial potential of human nature. But capitalism and the market economy could also founder because, without constraints and a moral lead from the top, they will ultimately disgust those (including many of the current beneficiaries) who are close to disaffection.

The free market system works, but it needs to work better than it is doing right now. One of the plus points of identity is that, nurtured intelligently, it can encourage a healthy sense of solidarity. As Charles Handy says in 'The Empty Raincoat': "We were not meant to stand alone. We need to belong - to something or someone. Only when there is a mutual commitment will you find people prepared to deny themselves for the good of others."

Programming people

The American anthropologist Edward T Hall defines 'culture' as "a system for creating, sending, storing and processing information". We are 'programmed', so to speak, by our environment, by the community within which we live. Geert Hofstede, the Dutch social psychologist, describes culture as "the software of the mind".

In his book 'The Language Instinct', Stephen Pinker provides an explicit definition of the phenomenon: "'Culture' refers to the process whereby particular kinds of learning contagiously spread from person to person in a community and minds become coordinated into shared patterns".

Indeed the ultimate determinant of human character is neither nationality nor genes, and certainly not language. It is culture, the culture of the immediate environment in which a person is brought up, and of which language is only a part.

Every culture - which means every country, every community - establishes its own rules, expressed in terms of values, ways of reasoning, behavioural traits, many of them unspoken and unrecorded. Those who consistently fail to respect these rules risk ostracism or eviction.

While there is ample proof of the power of culture, for both good and bad, there is just as conclusive evidence of its potential transferability in the right conditions and therefore, by implication, its arbitrariness.

One example is provided by the many cases of Belgian families - let's be more specific, Brussels francophone bourgeois families - that have adopted Vietnamese orphan children. The result is young adults that still look Vietnamese, but think and behave like... Brussels francophone bourgeois.

Culture is a phenomenon that is described very elegantly by Doris Lessing in her collection of lectures, 'Prisons We Choose To Live Inside'. In her words, "we are all of us, to some degree or another, brainwashed by the society we live in. We are able to see this when we travel to another country, and are able to catch a glimpse or our own country with foreign eyes. There is nothing much we can do about this except to remember that it is so. Every one of us is part of the great comforting illusions, and part illusions, which every society uses to keep up its confidence in itself. These are hard to examine, and the best we can hope for is that a kindly friend from another culture will enable us to look at our culture with dispassionate eyes."

It is ultimately culture, the sharing and the reliving of myriad common influences, that gives expression to the distinctiveness of a people. Today, even if this was not always the case, cultures and nation-states are viewed as concomitant. But just as culture reinforces the identity of the nation-state, it can also give expression to the lives of the state's various regions.

Defining the nation-state

Here, another definition is due: what constitutes a nation-state? This is the kind of intellectual challenge that creates as much heat as light, like the theological debate about the sex of angels or the number of them you could get on a pinhead. Many eminent historians and political scientists have applied their minds to this weighty issue.

For a start, however it is defined, there can be no question that the nation-state is a reality in the lives of everyone - and not just those of us Europeans whose predecessors invented the concept. Despite all the misery it has brought to Europe in particular, the nation-state rates as a highly successful formula. According to UN figures, there were 185 of them in the world at the beginning of 1996.

A sense of nation, in the modern interpretation of the word, certainly goes back no further than the middle of this millenium. However the French had laid the foundation stone for what was later to become nationalism as early as 987 AD - helped along by the bloody subjugation, and eventual annihilation, of the *langue d'oc* culture of southern France by the Capetian dynasty at the beginning of the 13th century.

As Eric Hobsbawm points out, it is also not unrealistic to think of Spain's Kingdom of Castile in the 15th century as a nation-state.

But the first real evidence of a national consciousness emerged in the 16th century with the English (it was difficult to talk of the British at the time). With the demise of feudalism and the ascendency of the House of Tudor, they decided not only that they were a cut above the rest, but that they were also a nation.

Hugh Seton-Watson, a contemporary British historian, believes this spontaneous nature of nationalism to be its chief characteristic: to create a nation, you have to have enough people who sense a common interest and behave accordingly. Period.

Despite its current status in the hearts and minds of many people, the nation-state is a recent creation. Most historians and political scientists consider that, in the modern and European sense of the term, it emerged with the French Revolution in 1789.

In his book 'Nations and Nationalism since 1780', Eric Hobsbawm offers a comprehensive definition of the modern concept of the nation-state:

"The characteristic modern state, receiving its symptomatic shape in the era of the French revolutions, though in many ways anticipated by the evolving European principalities of the sixteenth-seventeenth centuries, was novel in a number of respects. It was defined as a (preferably continuous and unbroken) territory over all of whose its inhabitants it ruled, and separated by clearly distinct frontiers or borders from other such territories. Politically it ruled over and administered these inhabitants directly, and not through intermediate systems of rulers and autonomous corporations. It sought, if at all possible, to impose the same institutional and administrative arrangements and laws all over its territory, though after the Age of Revolution, no longer the same religious or secular-ideological ones. And increasingly it found itself having to take notice of the opinions of its subjects or citizens, because its political arrangements gave them a voice - generally through various kinds of elected representatives - and/or because the state needed their practical consent or activity in other ways, e.g. as tax-payers or as potential conscript soldiers. In short, the state ruled over a territorially defined 'people' and did so as the supreme 'national' agency of rule over its territory, its agents increasingly reaching down to the humblest inhabitant of the least of its villages."

Hobsbawm makes the point that the emphasis on linguistic and cultural community was a 19th-century innovation, as was the term 'nationalism' itself!

For the French the concept of the nation is associated with the political idea of *liberté*, for the Germans it is the historical and linguistic concept of *Das Volk*. For the Russians it is sustained partly by the Orthodox religion, partly by the sense of a common cause when threatened from outside. Every nation has its own interpretation.

John Stuart Mill, the British philosopher, identified two key constituents of nationality: first, the wish quite simply to be governed together; second, the "common sympathy" emanating from a shared history, language or ideal.

In the early days of the nationhood process - when the thought was probably not in the minds of those deliberately or accidentally responsible for the political act itself, if they ever thought of it - the intelligentsia of these emerging nation-states rationalised the development as a pragmatic and in all probability transitory phenomenon on the road to a new world order.

They justified the new nation-states in terms of the administrative and economic benefits they brought to their citizens in an age dedicated to free trade. They accordingly spoke of a 'threshold principle', arguing that some potential states were too small to reap such benefits - the same argument that could be applied today to a Europe of the Regions.

Such thinking made a lot of sense. The nation-state is a product of evolutionary pressures, like mankind itself. But the problem today, with the apparatus in the hands of a ruling elite, is that the evolutionary process is in danger of stopping, despite the good intentions expressed by Europe's political classes in their support for the European Union.

Danilo Turk, a professor of international law at Slovenia's University of Ljubljana, is someone who is keenly and directly involved in the question of what constitutes a nation. He maintains there are three legal criteria: first, territory (nb not total surface area: "one thing that doesn't matter for sure is size", says Mr Turk); second, population; third, adequate state power to implement and defend the area's sovereignty.

Curiously, Mr Turk does not evoke the criterion of economic sufficiency. Presumably, in the case of Slovenia, this will be taken care of by accession to the European Union and access to the Single Market.

Of sovereignty and self-righteousness

Nationalism, at least in its nastier emanations, is easy to decry. Yet what lies behind it, the concept of sovereignty, is still regarded as a virtue.

Sovereignty is defined in my dictionary as "supreme and independent power". It therefore falls into the domain of those things that one can best describe as a self-affirmation ("look, that's the way it is..."). It is a weasel word *par excellence*, almost as weaselish as that Vatican-inspired bit of sophistry that is now so fashionable: subsidiarity.

The concept of sovereignty also brings in its train the sacred principle of non-intervention by any other authority, including a Higher One. This is a two-way street since, if appeals to sovereignty fail to do the trick, the next invocation is likely to be God himself, if it isn't Freedom...

But sovereignty also has a more sinister implication, namely the demands of loyalty it places on the individual. Loyalty is a vital yet fragile component of human society, particularly when it involves personal relationships. The charge of treason, the institutionalised version of human treachery, is still today a very emotive issue for a lot of people.

No wonder this powerful catalyst of institutionalised passions - appeals to sovereignty, scaremongering by the state, whatever the target - is open to abuse by governments even today, with some recent instances involving partial or total suspension of judgement and commonsense.

Even the Labour Party felt obliged to support the British government's ridiculous non-cooperation policy over the mad-cow issue. Any opposition would have incurred the risk of being construed as disloyalty to the national cause, a guaranteed vote-loser.

The rights of sovereignty of a nation-state - and, God help us, the increasingly promiscuous claims to subsidiarity, which might be better dubbed the NIMBY (Not In My Back Yard) principle - are inevitably conditional on that state's legitimacy.

As recently as 1956, a German federal court refused to indict an ex-SS officer accused of war crimes on the grounds that he had upheld "the right of the state to maintain itself"...

The concept of loyalty has been very seriously put to the test in recent European history. One country's traitor is another country's martyr. Even roles can change with the collapse of political systems, as was evident with *Die Wende* in Germany.

The former so-called German Democratic Republic was one of the states that ultimately had its legitimacy challenged, and rightly so. Since then some of its most loyal supporters, heroes of the socialist revolution, have been tried by the courts like common criminals.

Yet one of the most bizarre and tragic cases was that of the Soviet soldiers who refused to fire on the East German building workers demonstrating alongside the Brandenburg Gate in 1953. Found guilty of failing to obey orders, their act of decency was rewarded by execution at the hands of a Soviet firing squad.

An even more bizarre case, though happily not involving human lives, is described by Doris Lessing: "A certain tree was once sentenced to death, at the end of the last war. The tree was associated with General Pétain, for a time considered

France's saviour, then France's betrayer. When Pétain was disgraced, the tree was solemnly sentenced and executed for collaborating with the enemy."

Now, if that doesn't demonstrate the madness in men's minds, what does? It suggests to me there is something wrong not only with the individuals concerned, but with the concept and role of the nation-state. Loyalty should be to the human race (and to trees!), and not to a parochial authority determined by the arbitrary application of dotted lines.

In the past, in the name of the state, Germans have been gassed, Italians fed with castor oil, Spaniards have had their heads put in plastic bags, Frenchmen have been given electric shocks, Britons have been sent to the firing squad - all in the defence of a system convinced of its self-righteousness.

At least things have improved since the Middle Ages when traitors were successively hanged, cut down half-choked, disembowelled, castrated and, finally, buried alive or cut in four. Violence, intimidation and, as a by-product, fear have been powerful aids in the establishment and enforcement of national sovereignty. Stalin's purges are one example among many.

But in one respect the nation-state has served us well. It has given us with the framework for the establishment of principles of liberal democracy that we today take for granted - and that are, today, under threat from the very institutions that are supposed to defend them!

Historical hijackings

Ownership claims also extend to works of art that ought to be regarded as the patrimony of mankind. One of the longest-standing disputes relates to the Elgin marbles which were hijacked by a British ambassador, with the full agreement of the Turks, from a Greece which, at the time, was a backwater of the Ottoman Empire.

More recently, the treasures of King Priam of Troy have been the focus of an international squabble involving the Russians, the Germans, the Greeks and the Turks. In yet another recent incident, a Palestinian university professor was prepared to avow that his heritage "has a Jewish component" in order to justify claims to some obviously Hebrew artefacts!

A variation on this theme was provided by the discovery of the mummified body of a Bronze Age hunter in a glacier on the Austro-Italian frontier. Competitive Austrian and Italian claims to the find were checkmated by the separatist-minded and German-speaking 'Italians' of the South Tyrol who insisted he was a Tyrolean.

In the words of Peter Millar, a columnist with 'The European' newspaper, "to 'nationalise' mankind's early history is the sort of narrow-thinking that typifies totalitarian rather than liberal democratic attitudes." Yes, sir!

Of Race, Language, Religion and Class

"It is worth stressing at the outset that, while the language of race - gens, natio, 'blood', 'stock', etc. - is biological, its medieval reality was almost entirely cultural"

Robert Bartlett, *'The Making of Europe'*

"The populations of large territorial nation-states are almost invariably too heterogeneous to claim a common ethnicity, even if we leave aside modern immigration"

Eric Hobsbawm, *'Nations and Nationalism Since 1780'*

"It seems that the ideas which a nationalistic society, on the European model, has about its past are not only most dangerous when they are erroneous, but also most powerful. The concept of pure races has long been rejected by anthropologists, who think of human types as conveyors of bundles of heritages which are recombined in every generation"

E Esteyn Evans, *'The Personality of Ireland'*

"Race and ethnicity are the most minor differences of all. The human geniticists Walter Bodmer and Luca Cavalli-Sforza have noted a paradox about race. Among laypeople, race is lamentably salient, but for biologists it is virtually invisible. Eighty-five percent of human genetic variation consists of the differences between one person and another within the same ethnic group, tribe or nation"

Stephen Pinker, *'The Language Instinct'*

"The links between religion and national consciousness can be very close, as the examples of Poland and Ireland demonstrate"

Eric Hobsbawm, *'Nations and Nationalism Since 1780'*

"Were it not originally for religion, there would be little basis for Serbo-Croat enmity"

Robert D Kaplan, *'Balkan Ghosts'*

E ven 500 years ago, there were few communities in Europe that could reasonably claim, had they wanted to, to be ethnically homogeneous. In fact, they had better things to do with their time. In the intervening half-millenium, those communities that could have made this assertion have seen their claims made even more tenuous by migration and miscegenation.

The only western European peoples who seem to have a clear claim today to some degree of ethnic purity are the Basques and the Finns. Yet even the Finns are descended from three separate tribes, and share their country with a substantial Swedish minority.

Maybe the Swabians - descendants of one of the Alemanni tribes, the Suevi, today's Swabians - also have a case. Poachers turned gamekeepers, they won the right from an enfeebled Roman Empire to guard its frontiers. The consequence today is a community of common origin that extends along both banks of the Rhine through four countries from France's Alsace to the Austrian Vorarlberg.

But these are the exceptions. Less than 10 per cent of the 185 countries in the world today are ethnically homogeneous. Elsewhere we are confronted with one of two realities: a political entity, i.e. a state, which is shared by a number of ethnic groups, or an ethnic group which is shared by a number of countries. How inconvenient for the purists!

Even Hungary, long considered an ethnic island of sorts in a sea of Slavs and Germanics, is a challenge to the concept of racial homogeneity. At the end of the last century, less than half the population of the country spoke Magyar. More recently, in the early-1990s, a study undertaken jointly by a Budapest research institute and a German university identified 17 different racial groups, including more than one Magyar strain, Armenians, Ruthenians, Croats, Swabians (a splinter group who came down the Danube to repopulate areas laid waste by the Turks as they retreated), and Gypsies.

According to Luigi Barzini, the Italian author and politician, almost half the inhabitants of present-day France are the descendants of Germanic tribes. Italy saw the settlement of the 'longbearded people', today's Lombards, and the shortlived incursion of the Ostrogoths, who sacked Rome.

The Iberian peninsula provided the setting for a series of Germanic civilisations: first and fleetingly the Vandals, who gave their name to Andalusia, later the Suevi (them again) and the Visigoths. Spain was a very cosmopolitan place. Other settlers in that particular piece of God's Earth, some temporary but most of them permanent, included the Iberians, Celts, Phoenicians, Greeks, Romans, Carthaginians, Arabs, English and French.

The Celts, because they ended up in the most inaccessible corners of western Europe - Scotland, Ireland, the Isle of Man, Wales, Cornwall, Brittany, Galicia and northern Portugal - have managed to maintain some sort of ethnic identity. Yet even the most idiosyncratic of the Celts, the Irish, cannot evoke their Celtishness beyond the limits of their cultural traditions.

E Esteyn Evans, a Welshman and the author of an insightful book on Ireland, believes that the genes coming from English settlers there exceed those deriving from the Celts, and that "those coming from older stocks would constitute the largest proportion" (a reference to the earlier Upper Palaeolithic, Mesolithic and Neolithic settlers).

Many communities arrive at apparent homogeneity through a gradual process of miscegenation combined, in some cases, with their relative isolation. Portugal is a good example, but in its case as in so many others the *brassage* is like a minestrone soup, where one spoonful looks just like another, yet each spoonful contains enough ingredients to confound any claims to homogeneity.

Split and schism

The case of Bosnia is both an extreme one - and one that is still very fresh in the minds of everybody. Depending on whom you talk to, the country was a human paradise where different cultures cohabited and mingled, or it was a bomb waiting for the first hint of unrest.

Some people, the author included, were duped into thinking that the whole of Bosnia-Herzegovina was a lesson in multicultural harmony for all - multicultural, not multiracial, because most of the people involved were related ethnically in any case.

There is no more complex geopolitical case in European history than the old Yugoslavia. It all goes back to the end of the third century AD, when the Emperor Diocletian set in motion the partition of the Roman Empire between the Latin-speaking domains of the West and the Greek-speaking Byzantine empire of the East.

He then retired to his palace in a city appropriately called Split and is reputed to have spent the rest of his life cultivating cabbages, either there or in the neighbouring Roman settlement of Salona.

This was the first of a series of distinctly historical - and rather arbitrary - events that were ultimately to have serious consequences for contemporary politics. In the 11th century, Pope Leo IX and the Byzantine emperor Michael Cerularius, through an act of mutual excommunication, speeded the schism between the Roman and Orthodox churches and opened the way to the introduction of separate alphabets.

Already by the year 760 AD, the people of this part of the world had earned the definition of 'southern Slavs'

('Yugoslavs' in the Slav language), even if it wasn't used at the time. The Bavarian Duchy - a remote dependency of the Frankish emperors that by this time extended into today's Austria - established a protectorate over the Slavs on its eastern border. This, plus the decision of the previously footloose Magyars to settle in the Carpathian basin toward the end of the 10th century, had the effect of splitting the South Slavs of the Balkans, the Yugoslavs, from the other Slavic tribes to the north.

But the real story starts later. The 14th century saw the expansion of the Ottoman Turk dynasty westwards. The South Slavs found themselves in the frontline of Christianity. The first to face the Islamic onslaught, the most easterly of the Yugoslavs, were the Serbs.

They put up a brave fight on St Vitus' Day in the year 1389, and lost. The site of the battle was the 'Field of Black Birds', Kosovo Polje. This plain, as sad as Waterloo, was to be the scene of three more major battles over the next 500 years. No wonder it looms large in Serb mythology.

This epic Christian defeat is linked in the minds of all Serbs with the concept of a Greater Serbia and a visceral dislike of anything associated with the Islamic faith, Bosnian Muslims included. The idea that the Serbs had sacrificed their finest to save the rest of Christian Europe has been nurtured from that day, 600 years ago, to this.

Described by Rebecca West in her wonderful book 'Black Lamb and Grey Falcon' as "an incantatory poem", the Kosovo epic has since been legitimised, institutionalised and kept alive by generations of poets, writers and academics, including some university professors known to anyone who reads the papers. In short, it looks like a national conspiracy, but its roots go very deep into the Serbian collective subconscious.

The injustices of history

In his book 'The War in Eastern Europe' John Reed said of the Serbs in the First World War that "every peasant soldier knows what he is fighting for. When he was a baby, his mother greeted him, 'Hail, little avenger of Kossovo'[sic]".

Of course, a number of regrettable things have happened since Kosovo to justify the Serbs in their interpretation of history. They persisted courageously in their resistance to Ottoman domination. Then, for a change threatened from the north and west by the Austro-Hungarian Empire, they were treated to all manner of machinations and perfidies by the imperial authorities.

In the First World War, the Serbs heroically held off the Austrian and Bulgarian armies, nearly succumbed to a fierce epidemic, yet finally came back the victors. In the Second World War, the Croat fascist Ustase murdered millions of their people. Afterwards, Tito suppressed any nationalist impulses, Serb or other, in the name of national unity.

Whatever one may think of the Serbs, one has to concede them the right to feel keenly the glories, and particularly the injustices, of their history.

"Serbian nationalism", says American journalist Blaine Harden, "draws on an abiding feeling of victimization and historical injustice, obsessively recalling that Serbs have been conquered and butchered by Ottoman Turks, Germans and Croats [what about the Austrians?]. It teaches that the very survival of the Serbs is threatened by a conspiracy of Roman Catholic, Islamic and imperialistic enemies."

Now, the irony of all this - and perhaps the biggest irony in European history - is that ethnically the Serbs, the Croats and most of the Bosnian Muslims are one and the same people. They are all South Slavs, Yugoslavs.

Culture is a matter of nurture, not nature. Yet blood and genes still have a habit of getting in the way, more often than not without reason. Southeastern Europe is particularly strong on this score. The people of what used to be called Yugoslavia invoke their genetic differences all the time, yet the Serbs, the Croats and even a large proportion of the Bosnian Muslims are blood-brothers, whether they like it or not. The Greeks make a great deal of their Hellenism, yet their links with the people of Ancient Greece are as much surmise as scientific fact.

While directing the European Human Genome Diversity Project, Sir Walter Bodmer, a genial British scientist, set out to investigate the incidence of an inherited blood disorder, thalassaemia, on the island of Cyprus where 'Greek Cypriots' and 'Turkish Cypriots' cohabit uneasily. His carefully controlled study showed that the disorder was shared equally by both 'races', a conclusion that has disturbing socio-political implications for the people concerned. He announced the results to some Cypriot Greek Orthodox monks in a conversation which, in synthesis, went something like this:

Sir Walter: *"There's one type of thalassaemia common to Cyprus."*

First Cypriot: *"It's different from other types in the world?"*

Sir Walter: *"Yes, it's commoner than it is in Greece or Turkey."*

Second Cypriot: *"Couldn't you prove we descended from ancient Greeks?"*

Sir Walter: *"You're a little different, an older population..."*

Second Cypriot (confused): *"So you think we just feel Greek culturally?"*

Sir Walter: *"You're all Cypriots, Greek or Turkish, one people."*

First Cypriot (even more confused): *"It's very surprising to hear it."*

Sir Walter: *"It is."*

Reality can be uncomfortable when it challenges myths...

Those awful dotted lines - the ones that were so arbitrarily set at the Treaty of Versailles (see pages 14-15) - even find their way into Bosnian humour, despite the fact there has been little to laugh about.

Bosnian jokes frequently feature a comic couple, Mujo and Suljo, and a Golden Fish that grants wishes. Here is an example:

"Mujo and Suljo go fishing and catch a Golden Fish. 'If you set me free', says the fish, 'I will grant you a wish'.

'Can you get the Serbs to approve the new map of Bosnia?', asks Mujo. 'I'm tired of this war!'

The fish spreads the map out and looks at it carefully. 'I'm sorry', he says, 'it's impossible! Ask me something else.'

'OK', says Suljo. 'Can you make my wife, Fata, beautiful?' He brings Fata into the room.

'Hang on', says the Golden Fish, taking a quick glance, 'Let's have another look at that map...'."

In the words of a British historian, Nevill Forbes: "The Serbs and the Croats were, as regards race and language, originally one people, the two names having merely geographical signification." It was initially, and still essentially, religion that got in the way. Today these divisions are reinforced by competitive claims to real estate.

In fact, on the basis of anteriority, the Serbs have no claim to Bosnia at all. Most of them arrived, by invitation, in the 16th and 19th centuries. The Croats have been in the area since the seventh century.

Many of the Bosnian Muslims were converts to Islam, precisely because they were persecuted as heretics by the Roman Catholic church: their religion, Bogomilism, was later to erupt throughout western Europe as the Cathar heresy. The only significant exceptions are those Muslims who are ethnically Albanian, descendants of the ancient Illyrians.

So the issue is not race, not even language: the Serbs and Croats share basically the same vocabulary, the difference being in the scripts (the Serbs inherited the Cyrillic alphabet from the Orthodox church). The issue is a fiery blend of culture, religion and real estate.

Class comes into the equation too, much as it has contributed to the squabblings between Flemings and Walloons in modern Belgium. In his book 'Balkan Ghosts' Robert D Kaplan talks about "Sarajevo, where Croats, Serbs, Muslims, and Jews had traditionally lived together in reasonable harmony. But the villages all around were full of savage hatreds, leavened by poverty and alcoholism".

Indeed the backwoodsman mentality typical of Bosnian Serbs compares starkly with the urban sophistication of their Muslim neighbours. This may be explained in part by the fact that many of the latter belonged to a landowning elite that, as Bogomil heretics, chose to 'convert' to Islam to escape the persecution of the Christian churches.

With the ready acquiescence of their Turkish masters, these Bosnian Muslims continued to exercise lordship over the Christian peasantry long after feudalism had died out elsewhere in Europe. Latterly, Tito kept the lid on the Yugoslav cauldron for nearly forty years but, ten years after his death, it boiled over.

Despite three years of vicious warfare, Sarajevo reasserted its erstwhile reputation for tolerance when, on Christmas Eve 1995, Muslims joined Christians in the city's Catholic cathedral for midnight mass. They were paying tribute to the mutual respect that had enabled Catholics, Orthodox Christians, Muslims and Jews to live in harmony for many centuries. But the spirit of Sarajevo belies the experience of Bosnia, pre- and post-Dayton, as a whole. With the events of recent years, the 'Us & Them' syndrome is more deeply ingrained than ever.

That rank outsider to the south, the Former Yugoslav Republic of Macedonia (FYROM), may yet provide us with an object lesson in how to sustain a heterogeneous society. Despite the theatrical posturings of the previous Greek government and others, this modest little community has kept a cool, clear head and is putting the principle of a multicultural and religiously pluralistic society into practice.

Dotted lines, faultlines

So-called racial conflict is rarely just a matter of race, if it is even a matter of race at all. In many cases a number of catalysts are at work.

One of the most powerful is religion. Add this to the 'mix' and the result is a heady and, as often as not, decidedly toxic brew which dissipates the fundamental precept of respect for life that religions are supposed to instill.

In the words of Gene Deitch, a Czech citizen, "religion, which is supposed to elevate humankind to a higher level of consciousness and to promote brotherhood, in fact divides people." And, he adds, "I suggest that we generate a world-wide Hate-the-Martians movement"...

It is extraordinary how religion, supposedly promoting the Christian principles of forgiveness and reconciliation, has contributed so much to the process of setting peoples against one another. Tragic examples are Yugoslavia and Northern Ireland.

In the case of Ulster, the descendants of the Protestant 'planters' found a worthy adversary in a Catholic community that in fact had only discovered a new identity in religion in the 19th century due to a combination of factors: the impact of the Great Famine, the vacuum left by the impoverishment of the native Celtic language and heritage, a growing and centralised bureaucracy, and a new spirit of morality.

While religious practice is on the wane in the European west - though enjoying a revival in the east - religion, like land hunger and politics, has drawn its own lines across the map of Europe. Not just dotted lines, but major faultlines.

The biggest faultline of all is the one that runs down through what used to be Yugoslavia and which owes its origins to the schism between the Roman and the Orthodox Christian churches. Robert Bartlett comments in his book 'The Making of Europe' that "even today one of the sharpest cultural divisions in the Slavic world is between those peoples who were converted by Germans and those converted by Greeks".

Then there is another faultline, though of diminishing significance: the one between Catholic and Protestant Europe. And then, of course, there are lots of little 'dotted lines'.

Some of them, like the Catholic/Protestant dividing line in the southern Netherlands, split countries in two - although it has to be conceded that the 'pluralistically conformist' Dutch, whose Catholicism has always had a Calvinist flavour, have achieved a positively ecumenical level of religious symbiosis.

Others reinforce the political dotted lines, as in the case of the Lutheranism of Norway, the Calvinism of Switzerland and the Jesuit tradition of Austria - all of which mark the peoples' mentality, just as the peoples' mentality, I suggest, helped determine their choice of religion (in fairness to the Austrians, they had their Catholicism forced on them by the Counter-Reformation).

In most cases the effects of religious influence are benign. But, when caught up in other issues like social privilege or historical injustice, religion can be the catalyst for something malevolent.

The case of Yugoslavia started out as a product of politics, confirmed in religion and sustained by myth, but religion must bear much of the responsibility. The Serbian Orthodox church kept, and still keeps, the memory of its national heroes alive by canonising them and featuring them in its daily liturgy. It shoulders the same responsibility as all the other Orthodox churches, namely not just to protect but to actively promote the interests of the nation-state to which it belongs. Revitalised, the Russian Orthodox Church is becoming suspiciously chauvinistic.

In such cases, religion ultimately qualifies as race. Many observers also point out that the Orthodox Church throughout eastern Europe is viscerally anti-western.

There are still Orthodox churches which openly espouse discrimination, as many have found out to their cost, among them an American author, Thomas Butler, who spoke of Orthodox-Catholic prejudice as a powerful force: "A few years ago, I visited the Orthodox monastery of Iviron on Mount Athos in Greece. While I was attending the early morning liturgy, a monk approached and asked whether I was Orthodox or Catholic. When I replied 'Catholic', he told me to 'go outside and pray'."

A recent witness to the fact that such intolerance is reciprocated by Catholics is Slavko Curuvija, a Serb journalist: "Croats are having their past checked for the slightest drop of 'impure' Serbian blood. Those who do not flee keep eyes in the back of their heads and talk in whispers. They are converting from the Orthodox to the Catholic faith and change their names and surnames to hide Serbian origins."

The fiercer face of religion is certainly not confined to Europe. We have seen it in the assassination of Yitzhak Rabin by a member of a right-wing Jewish sect and in the violence of Muslim fundamentalists.

In the case of the latter, it can at least be said that their militancy owes something to the intolerance shown by the Roman Church in general, and the Catholic monarchs of Castile and Leon in particular, toward the relatively tolerant Moors in the first half of the present millenium. More recent European nation-state intervention in the affairs of the Middle East has added massively to this resentment.

The curse of class

Despite religion's capacity to divide rather than reconcile, in the last two centuries class differences have been an even greater catalyst of nationalist tendencies. Very often they go hand-in-hand. The pressures of internal struggles within communities were usefully channelled, as it seemed at the time, into ideologies which contributed to the emergence of nationalism in many countries in Europe.

The Belgian squabble owes nothing to genetics. It isn't even exclusively a matter of culture. It is a heady mixture of language and class, with religion thrown in for good measure in the sense that, even today, the Flemish tend to be religious and the Walloons not.

It is precisely because the need for a common identity - what becomes a sense of nationhood - drives people to draw on as many alibis as possible that the end-product is so dangerous. With the addition of mythmaking, either in the collective subconscious or deliberately inspired by politicians, public opinion is sufficiently misled to be totally confused without ever knowing it.

Clear thinking is no friend of separatism. In Northern Ireland culture is confused with religion, in Flanders language is mixed in with historical class divisions, in Spain history is caught up in political preferences, the Catalans and Basques being to the left of the Castilian centre. It doesn't suit anyone to unravel this intellectual and emotional tangle.

Resentment of other peoples' class attitudes and privileges has poisoned relations between communities over the course of history. It is a resentment that has been felt for nearly a millenium by the Slovaks towards their traditional Hungarian masters (with the consequences we see today for the Hungarian minority in Slovakia), by the Finns towards their Swedish elite, and by the Czechs towards the Austrians. The solution for the upwardly mobile has been to assimilate with the class detested by aping its language and habits. This the Czechs did with great assiduity.

The class issue in France - since the Revolution the most vocal though not the most committed champion of the principle of equality - was and still is the gulf between the privileged and the rest. In other countries in recent times the process has been more complex. The local versions of nationalism in 19th-century Croatia, Catalonia and Flemish Belgium, and more recently in Germany's Weimar Republic, were and still are largely the product of the aspirations of an emerging lower middle class.

Involved in a class struggle within their own society or sensing an immediate or potential threat to their security, and lacking an identity of their own, these people found refuge in the new religion of nationalism. The lower middle classes were the breeding ground.

Royalty was always international - how many Britons remember that, until the beginning of this century, the House of Windsor was called the House of Guelph (i e. Welf)? - and much of the establishment, including the intelligentsia, equally so. The working classes had better things to do with their time.

The catalyst that creates nationalism has many ingredients, not the least of which is insecurity or fear. The issues are never clear-cut. Theories of racial or cultural uniqueness, some largely mythological, blend with religion or class consciousness, differences in language, and other factors like cuisine and colour of skin. No wonder the threat of nationalism is always there!

The Atavists

"The noblest countries - England, France, Italy - are those where the blood is most mixed. Germany is no exception"

Ernest Renan

"When nations have existed for a long and glorious time, they cannot break with their past, whatever they do; they are influenced by it at the very moment when they work to destroy it; in the midst of the most glaring transformation, they remain fundamentally in character and destiny such as their history has formed them"

François Guizot, French statesman

"It seems that the ideas which a nationalistic society, on the European model, has about its past are not only most dangerous when they are erroneous, but also most powerful"

E Estyn Evans, 'The Irish Heritage'

"I see no reason why the people of this country should have to change the habits of a lifetime, and of generations, just because we are members of the European Community"

Junior British Transport Minister defending the principle of driving on the left

"Britain will resemble the orchestra at the end of one of the Marx Brothers' films, playing sublimely but unaware that it was drifting out to sea"

Sir Roy Denman

"The primitive ferocity of Greek nationalism, which is a sign of Greek insecurity, has bared its teeth again"

'The Economist', 22/5/1993

"How do you divide up the past?"

Gane Todorovski, Skopje poet

Ernest Renan forgot to mention Spain, but he was right in what he said. Mongrel civilisations tend to be intelligent and creative ones. What a pity, then, that they use this intelligence and creativity to conjure up national identities and myths to compensate for their uncertain origins.

English society - 'British' is not a cultural definition - has always survived on myths. The most pernicious of these find expression internationally in a sense of feeling different (partly justified!) and, domestically, in a sense of class. I have dealt with these phenomena at some length in earlier books, together with other ingredients like a love of tradition, a distaste for regulation, and the cult of the amateur.

Jane Kramer, perhaps the most perceptive transatlantic observer of the Old World, says this about my fellow-countryfolk in her book 'Europeans': "The English produced the most class-ridden society in Europe, and in some ways the most aggressively self-deluded - and for centuries managed to hold it together by pretending that responsible social co-operation was a natural expression of Englishness, rather than the protective accommodation of citizens to one another in a free country. Now that psychic space is gone."

Today, in Great Britain, maintaining the myths is one way of compensating for poor government. All British administrations since World War II have succeeded in unnerving the Great British Public by their incompetence - though the GBP has had lots of entertainment from the proceedings, particularly since the Lower House (an appropriate description!) went on TV.

More recently those in power have resorted to a blend of self-indulgence and schoolboy arrogance that has prompted one observer to describe them as "a distant, detested and self-interested class".

In some countries, France in particular, this would be enough to provoke a revolution (note that French revolutions tend, as the name implies, to go around in circles, ending up where they started from). In recent times the best the British have been able to do in the way of protest is the Campaign for Real Ale and, most topically, demonstrations in favour of animal rights or against motorway construction.

But even the GBP is beginning to wake up to the fact that something is wrong with its leaders, if they can be graced with the word. The Mother of Parliaments has been caught, time and again, with her knickers down. Not content with slamming the Opposition, government constantly resorts to alibi, hype and hypocrisy.

This kind of behaviour stands out in stark contrast to the vapid pretensions of those in power. No wonder the people no longer have any faith in their political institutions.

Not that the public has much opportunity to witness their work at first hand. Government has drained much of the responsibility, apparent or real, from the grassroots, sapping local government and concentrating power in Westminster.

As 'The Economist' commented in mid-1992: "Britain has a system of parliamentary absolutism which is centralised and unbalanced to a remarkable degree... The truth is that the British system, which its admirers laud as being peculiarly flexible and responsive, is rigid and slow to adapt to outside change." By 1996, encouraged by the revelations of the Scott report, the paper was even terser, speaking of "an obsessively secretive government machine, riddled with incompetence, slippery with the truth and willing to mislead Parliament."

Domestic duplicity has been matched by jingoism in foreign affairs, an art of which Mrs Thatcher was a past-mistress. Emerging triumphant from the 1990 Dublin Summit of the European Community, as it was then, she trumpeted "we won!" instead of saying something reasonable like "our point of view prevailed".

This kind of thinking is more appropriate to football championships. As it happens, she said it on the same day as the England-Belgium match in the World Cup, so perhaps she confused the two events.

Maggie has set English football fans a fine example, as events before and after the Euro 96 semi-finals showed. One chant, to the tune of the 'Camptown Lady', ran: "Two World Wars and one World Cup, doo dah, doo dah, two World Wars and one World Cup, doo dah doo dah day". But, when the Germans won, the English fans went on the rampage.

As Kirsty Hughes, a director at the Royal Institute of International Affairs, commented at the time: "It's very xenophobic. The war is over, but the inability of the British to let go of this imagery reflects the failure of Britain to find a new modern role in the Europe of the 20th century [this said in 1996!]. Britain keeps looking backwards because it is not confident of itself in the present and the future." Sad but true.

English MPs cry louder about subsidiarity than anyone else, yet fail to practise it in their own country - and not just in respect of the aspirations of the Scots and the Welsh. Not even the French can muster such Pavlovian responses as the English do, positively, to words like 'sovereignty' and 'subsidiarity' and, negatively, to a word like 'federalism' (the 'F-word').

In the words of the journalist Samuel Brittan, the country's sovereignty "has already been eroded ... by Britain's own elective dictatorship". To which I would add that squeals about losing sovereignty to an independent European Union central bank, when the Bank of England has for too long been a tool of short-term government policy far removed from the interests of the electorate, smack of total humbug.

Today, living in a country bereft of much of its real economic and political clout, Little Englanders simulate prestige with sentimental and ultra-fragile concepts like 'the balance of power' and 'the special relationship'.

The British press, mastered by ex-colonials, adds fuel to the flames by mounting scurrilous and poorly substantiated attacks on things like 'Brussels bureaucracy', 'German hegemony', foreigners in general and continentals in particular.

The same jingoistic spirit infused the mind of a British reader of the 'International Herald Tribune' when he wrote, in a letter to the editor: "We did not fight two world wars against Germany so that we could hand over monetary control of our country to the Bundesbank - no matter how efficient it may be".

As a Tory MP was heard to say recently to one of his German counterparts: "My dear chap, it has been Britain's role

---

How the British do things...

"I became chairman [of the Countryside Commission] as a consequence of sharing a cab with a stranger. Another quango* chairman was appointed following a pheasant shoot at which the secretary of state was a fellow gun; the subsequent chairman of a water authority bumped into a cabinet minister while birding on a Greek island [what kind of birds?]. It is a splendidly capricious and British way of doing things. I am advised that the success-failure rate is about the same as when headhunters are engaged. And look at the thousands of guineas you save". Guineas, eh?

Chairman of the Countryside Commission, a well-known British NGO, writing in his organisation's newsletter in 1991.

* quasi-autonomous non-governmental organisation

---

over the past 200 years to maintain the balance of power in Europe, and we've certainly no intention of giving up that role now." Is that the intention behind all the government's European chicanery?

Devolution or independence?

One of the things that the British Parliament will have to adapt to soon is Scottish insistence on devolution, even if on Westminster's terms. In the words of a Scots politician, "we are between the devil of devolution and the deep blue sea of independence".

The debate is fuelled by the fact that the Scots have a visceral hostility to the Tory Party which goes far deeper than anything felt in England. This may have something to do with history.

It also has a lot to do with the fact that Scotland is a more collectivist society than much of England, the North excepted, with a stronger community spirit. The fact that Mrs Thatcher said (another memorable utterance) "there is no such thing as society" certainly didn't endear her to the Scots.

In addition, in the words of Scots journalist Alan Massey: "The most noticeable feature of Scottish life over the past 20 years is the diminution of the sense of being British... First, the loss of empire. Scotland always thought itself to be an equal partner in the empire. That was satisfying. Then, the general decline of Britain. If you're a junior partner in a declining enterprise, that's not an effective position to be in."

To this has to be added a factor common to much of Europe today, namely the globalisation of life and the opening up of cultures to influences from outside. One of the latter is the European Union itself which, in the words of one observer, "has thrown some of the central features of the unmodern British state into sharp relief. It has increased, rather than weakened, a pre-existing Scottish sense of distinctiveness within the United Kingdom."

The result is a growing awareness among the Scots, an essentially sensible and realistic people, that something has to change. Consider the words used in the introduction to the manifesto published by the Scottish Constitutional Convention in November 1995: "Scotland approaches a new millenium facing a stark choice. It has a distinguished and distinctive structural heritage, evident in Scotland's legal system, its educational system, its social, cultural and religious traditions. These things are the very fabric of Scottish society, yet Scotland has come to lack democratic control over them. Their conduct is determined by a government for which few Scots voted, operating through a dense tangle of unelected quangos."

The Convention, like most Scots, is not looking for independence from England. The call is for a more democratic and direct positioning in the context of the European Union, to which the Scots show much greater attachment than their English neighbours, despite the distance between them and their continental colleagues. The Convention looks in particular to the example of "the popular and effective Parliaments now flourishing in various parts of Spain" (see chapter 7).

A Scottish parliament would have jurisdiction over health, education, law, social services, transport, housing, environment and various aspects of economic policy. Decisions on the things that matter most to Scots would thus, quite rightly, be brought closer to home.

A MORI opinion poll undertaken in Scotland in June 1996 showed that 66 per cent of voters wanted a Scottish parliament. Moreover 57 per cent would welcome a parliament even with tax-raising powers - never a popular idea with voters!

The Labour Party has already accepted the principle of local referenda on both Scottish and Welsh devolution. The Tory Party still seems to think that the Scots have reason to leave their destiny in the fumbling and fudgy hands of Westminster.

Speaking of the various factions active in Scots society, Tom Nairn of Edinburgh University's Department of Sociology says: "The result is curiously similar to the old dissident movements of Eastern Europe, although here the 'official' enemy is less a police state than an antiquated and London-oriented political order."

"The latter has become like a chrysalis out of which a whole complex of new tendencies is struggling to emerge, under the umbrella of civil or small 'n' nationalism."

"Behind it there is disenchantment with Westminster customs [what the Scottish Constitutional Convention calls 'the ritual confrontations of British politics'], or perhaps with traditional politics as such. Such feelings exist all over Britain and Europe."

Summing it up in the words of Christopher Harvie of the University of Tübingen, "the Scots regard themselves as a grown-up country shackled to an increasingly dotty parent".

Apparently the people of the Orkney Islands, even further north, share the feelings of the Scots but react differently. If Scotland seceded from the United Kingdom, the Orcadians might opt for union with Norway!

The British government's position on Scotland is in stark contrast to its readiness to contemplate a Northern Ireland assembly.

Quite understandably it would love to wash its hands of those pestiferous Ulstermen, who not only squander scarce national resources but also bring ridicule on that hallowed English institution, the bowler hat!

In the words of John Hume, the SDLP leader and one of the few sensible politicians in that crazy little corner of the British Isles: "Anyone who isn't confused in Northern Ireland doesn't really understand what is going on!".

The dottiest and the naughtiest

If despite keen competition from Ulstermen the English establishment is, to echo Christopher Harvie's description, the dottiest in western Europe - both pre and post the mad-cow saga - the French establishment certainly rates as the naughtiest.

Where the English wallow in nostalgia and tradition, the French trumpet their superiority to a world that, at best, takes no notice and, at worst, despises them for their lack of taste and discretion. Admittedly they do it tongue-in-cheek and, naively, they sometimes think they get away with it.

The concept of a nation is, both generically and individually, an ideological construct, the product of a process of self-awareness. No better example can be found than France itself, which emerged from a revolutionary ideology that created enough fervour to fire the imagination of its inhabitants into pursuing an ideal that brazenly challenged the realities. Nationalism *à la française* is relatively recent and largely synthetic.

In 1789 the country was a mass of different dialects and the people represented various ethnicities, essentially Germanic - and not Celtic as it suited the Revolution to present them. Moreover, France's frontiers with the interior of the continent were, to say the least, geographically incoherent.

More than half the inhabitants of France were not even able to sing Rouget de Lisle's new national anthem, the 'Marseillaise' because they couldn't speak the language. It is estimated that only 12-13 per cent of the population spoke it correctly and 50 per cent couldn't speak it at all (in both northern and southern France virtually no one spoke French).

No wonder the French have since been so insistent on linguistic uniformity. On the other hand, they have at last acknowledged the existence of "the Corsican people", which means that the man who contributed most to French history in the last two hundred years, Napoleon Bonaparte, wasn't even French!

Thanks to the spirit of the times, though, the ideology of 1789 prevailed and, especially in elite circles, is as powerful today as it was then. Added to an excess of dirigism and centrism this may contribute today, in much-changed circumstances, to the antagonism the provinces feel towards Paris.

Jane Kramer again: "History, in France, has a pedagogic function. It is only as 'true' as its usefulness in maintaining proper attitudes toward being French - including the fierce and oblivious identification Frenchmen have with France and with everything they mean by France. Strangers tend to see that identification as nationalism or chauvinism, but it is much more primitive than that. A Frenchman identifies with France the same way he lifts his chin and sticks out his lower lip when he is puzzled - as a kind of reflex action."

Ah, yes! - yet something is changing. As the evidence offered in chapter 8 suggests, the younger generations are finding an identity of their own, namely the difference between their value systems and those of their elders. Asked in a 1990 poll if they felt a greater affinity with a French person of their parents' age or a German of their own age, 60 per cent of French children responded "a German of my own age". Only 27 per cent opted for a French person of their parents' age.

French males, mature or not, have a great penchant for behaving like little boys - a proclivity that becomes more marked as one moves up the hierarchy, culminating in the Presidency. It is no surprise, therefore, that President Mitterand conducted a 15-minute televised interview marking the end of the Gulf War without once referring to the United States (he also never acknowledged the help he received from Britain in WWII).

Later, equally cynically - and maybe naively for someone who claimed to epitomise French vision and statesmanship - he took care not to call Gorbachev during the *putsch*.

As Luigi Barzini, the Italian journalist and author, says: "The main aim of French foreign policy is to flatter the people's high opinion of their country and prod them to accept the necessary disciplines and sacrifices".

In the words of 'The Economist', "more than any other European country, it [France] believes that influence abroad forms a central part of its national identity". Certainly recent French history has done a great job in persuading the individual to confuse his identity with that of the state - a mindset reinforced by French politicians' frequent references to *'La France'* and, in moments of panic, *'La Patrie'*.

On two consecutive days while writing these lines, I read of two separate incidents which illustrate perfectly both the French appetite for self-aggrandisement and its irrelevance to the modern world.

The first news item, in the 'International Herald Tribune', reported that the French had been frustrated in their attempt to have the Dayton Accord renamed the 'Elysée Treaty' on the pretext that the Bosnia-Herzegovina agreement hammered out in Ohio was being signed in the French presidential palace! Quite understandably the United States, aided and abetted by Britain, refused to condone this act of international piracy.

Despite taking his ideological distances from his predecessor, President Chirac followed Mitterand's example by later opting to take on world opinion over nuclear tests in the Pacific. Once a French *défi* has been made, it takes an awful lot of wild horses (or rioters in the streets) to get a French President to change his mind... not because he is President, but because he is President *and* French.

I say 'he' because, up till now, France has been a male-dominated society. It might be a good idea if the French were to elect a *Présidente* next time: she would certainly act more sensibly than her predecessors - even if Edith Cresson didn't as prime minister!

The second incident, reported in the same paper a day later, concerned French chicanery over the OECD's 1995 report on literacy skills. This found that France's adult population came low on the literacy scale, far behind Sweden, the Netherlands, Germany, Switzerland, Canada and the United States, and only slightly ahead of Poland.

In the words of the 'International Herald Tribune' again: "The French need not worry about being embarrassed by the report. When French officials studied its preliminary conclusions two months ago, they were so incensed that they insisted that all references to France be excised from the 200-page document...". An OECD official went on to say: "Only the French censored the results, which is tantamount to refusing to acknowledge the truth staring you in the face".

At least most thinking French people, of whom there are quite a lot, don't take themselves in when they think they're taking the rest of us in. As a French businessman puts it, "the French are logical, rational and Cartesian, but not to *do* logical things. It is only to be able to explain in an apparently logical way the illogical things they do."

To the credit of the French, their attachment to the principle of *jus soli*, reflecting their desire to keep their numbers up, has made them very sympathetic to people of foreign blood (even their fairy tales end "and they lived happily ever after and had lots of children!"). The government assumes that assimilation into French society is "the inevitable desire" of the immigrants. In fact births, marriages and naturalisations add more than 100,000 people of foreign parentage to the native French population every year.

Nationalism, as I hope I have explained elsewhere, can draw its inspiration from a range of sources. It's a question of horses for courses. The French put their money on the 'culture horse' because they wouldn't get far by backing the ethnic or any other version (despite their efforts to be different, they are just as human as anyone else). But, as so often in matters French, their determination to state their case emerges as a parody of their own very rich culture.

French chauvinism, with the emphasis on country and culture, is understandably fierce but equally irrational when it comes to the defence of the language. Take for example the words of a senate cultural affairs committee report published at the end of 1995: "France has a vocation to propose to its European partners an audacious linguistic project to the extent that our language supported by a prestigious past as well as a global diffusion... possesses a particular political dimension."

The infamous Loi Toubon banning the use of the English language in public life - 3,500 words were characterised as 'improper' at the time of its introduction - shows how uncartesian the cartesian French can be.

One aspect of this is the desperate promotion of *La Francophonie*, a cerebral community which recently welcomed Moldova, of all countries, to its midst. Another is the edict to all French popular radio stations, put into effect on New Year's Day 1996, that at least 40 per cent of all broadcasts between 6.30 am and 10.30 pm must be in the language of Molière or (ha ha!) a French dialect. Alsatian?

Who are the barbarians?

The French are right to want to protect their wonderful culture, but this is not the way to do it. At least, the measure is a little less cynical than one introduced by the Greeks which, in a blatantly protectionist initiative designed to help their own toy industry, only allows the screening of toy commercials on television after 10 o'clock at night! Admittedly Greek children stay up late...

National identity, not just national interest, is an issue that clearly preoccupies the Greeks enormously. Unlike their ancient homonyms, with whom they have little in common, today's Greeks lack anything sufficiently distinctive and coherent to make the issue relevant. Their relaxed attitude towards ethnic identification is demonstrated by the cavalier description of the Macedonians they acquired in 1913 as 'slavophone Greeks'.

This attitude is encouraged by the fact that, in this case, there is no clear identification with real estate. Pre-Alexander, classical Greece was a conglomeration of city-states. With Alexander, it became an empire which extended to India. Post-Alexander, it became part of someone's else's empire, Roman, Byzantine, then Ottoman. So the gap has had to be filled by an almost mystical sense of 'Greekitude' which is not even determined by language.

In his fine book 'Exploring the Greek Mosaic', Benjamin Broome expands this point: "Greek identity has never been a simple issue. It cannot be linked solely with language, as there were many Greeks living in Asia Minor or along the Black Sea coast until 1922 who spoke only Turkish, and until the beginning of this century there were pockets of

Greeks even in the Peloponnese who spoke Albanian or Slavic as their first language."

The classical Greeks didn't have to worry about this kind of thing. What they were was evident to everyone, including themselves, even if Philip of Macedonia's wife - Alexander the Great's mother - hailed from Epirus which, in terms of the modern map of Europe, straddles Albania as well as northwest Greece.

In any case Philip and Alexander were, as Macedonians, not exactly kosher by Athenian standards. No less than Demosthenes spoke of "Philip - a man who not only is no Greek, and in no way akin to the Greeks, but is not even a barbarian from a respectable country - no, a pestilent fellow of Macedon, a country from which we never even get a decent slave." In fact most of Alexander's Greek contemporaries viewed the Macedonian and his cohorts with fear and loathing: they had reason to do so since he snuffed out the fragile flame of Athenian democracy.

Yet brushing aside Demosthenes' judgement and the record of history, today's Greeks consider Philip and Alexander to be Greek enough by contemporary standards to justify all the fuss about FYROM, the Star of Vergina, etc. The rest of us are still barbarians...

Frankly, it all goes so far back in history - to a time more than two millenia ago, when there were no dotted lines on the map of Europe in any case - that it is difficult to understand what the fuss was all about. One of the most fussed was the late Melina Mercouri, who used all her questionable histrionic gifts to hype the issue beyond recognition. In parenthesis, I am proud to have a Greek friend who had the courage to tell her, to her face, that she couldn't act.

In his book 'Nations and Nationalism Since 1780', Eric Hobsbawm comments thus on the evolution of the Macedonia affair: "The inhabitants of Macedonia had been distinguished by their religion, or else claims to this or that part of it had been based on history ranging from the medieval to the ancient, or else on ethnographic arguments about common customs and ritual practices. Macedonia did not become a battlefield for Slav philologists until the twentieth century, when the Greeks, who could not compete on this terrain, compensated by stressing an imaginary ethnicity."

So hyped are official Greek attitudes that Michael Papadakis, an 18-year-old Greek student, was threatened in 1993 with a year's prison sentence for distributing a leaflet with the apparently incendiary words: "Macedonia belongs to its people. There are no races. We are all of mixed descent". Absolutely right.

Many modern Greeks demonstrate by their posturings that they do not share the self-confident identity of the Ancients. Accordingly they claim, with great vehemence and against all the evidence, direct lineage with the ancient Greeks.

I would not go so far as Fallmerayer, a 19th-century German scholar, who categorised the modern Greeks as Slav. Yet it is evident enough that there has been a great miscegenation process at work since classical times, with Levantines, Vlachs, Ottoman Turks and others all doing their bit!

Even Greeks, when they feel reasonable, will admit to their uncertain origins. The author Nicholas Gage, a Greek despite his name, concedes that for the most part "modern Greeks are the product of centuries of racial mixing, and the invasions by the Turks, Slavs, Franks, and Italians can be read in their faces".

Whatever they may be, modern Greeks are imbued with a mystical and largely mythical sense of national pride. The Greek government's climbdown in early-1996 over the Aegean islet of Imia - inevitably endowed with a different name, Kardak, by the Turks (that's another trick used by nationalists) - prompted the opposition leader, Miltiadis Evert, to say: "The removal of Greek troops and the lowering of the Greek flag constitutes an act of treason".

Not to be outdone Yannis Varvitsiotis, a former conservative defence minister, spoke for many but happily not all of his compatriots when he said: "I am overcome by the sense of shame that every Greek feels". In the Greek collective subconscious, memories of their eviction from Asia by the troops of Kemal Ataturk are still fresh in their minds.

"Pendeli, Greece - There could be no doubt about the passions of Father Timotheos.

Outside the medieval monastery, the priest's face lighted up only when he had reached the depths of the vaults.

'These are the secret classrooms', said the archimandrite or superior. He was showing the tiny alcoves where the monks used to run a hidden Greek school. Next, with evident pride, he opened up the old hiding place for gunpowder and weapons.

'I still have two guns', he confided and launched into tales of a heroic past in which Orthodox Christian monks defended their sites and kept the Greek language and religion alive during nearly 400 years of Turkish occupation, ending in the 19th century.

'And please accept my book', he continued, handing over a copy of 'Eternal Greece of Mine'. It carried the subtitle 'The Position and Brilliance of Greece in World History'."

Extract from article in the 'International Herald Tribune'

The 'Us & Them' Syndrome

"We naturally feel superior. The us-and-them psychology of groups being what it is, they probably think themselves superior to us too"

William H Cohen, 'The River That Flows Uphill'

"Nationalism is an emotive doctrine that commands vast support among any ethnic group that it purports to represent... If we are honest it must be admitted that a tyranny of a majority can be as bad as the tyranny of one man"

Letter to 'The Economist'

"Everyone is right in trying to preserve his or her vernacular tongue, without which one feels deprived of roots and identity. But this should not exclude other languages"

Marqués de Tamarón

"A state which is incompetent to satisfy different races condemns itself; a state which labours to neutralise, to absorb or to expel them is destitute of the chief basis of self-government"

Lord Acton

"Xenophobia has become the most widespread mass ideology in the world"

Eric Hobsbawm

"Look around Europe and you will find happy minorities in federal or sort-of-federal mosaics"

The Economist, 23/9/1995

"The triumph of culture is to overpower nationality"

Ralph Waldo Emerson

Europe has had a history of mass movements from the *Völkerwanderungen* of the first millenium to the westwards movement of millions since the breaching of the Berlin Wall.

As long as emigration and immigration went relatively unhindered, the minorities issue took care of itself. You solved the minority problem in one country by creating an immigration problem in another. But that has now changed, with the belated reaction of western governments to the flood of peoples from the south and the east. It is estimated that official requests for asylum filed with European Union member states fell from a record high of nearly 675,000 in 1992 to less than half that in 1995.

The least that can be said about frontiers - drawing dotted lines across the map of Europe - is that they are untidy. They are inevitably a compromise with reality, and somebody always gets hurt in the process. If we had no frontiers, we would mathematically have a lot less minorities, with all the problems they represent.

In the context of European history, discrimination against minorities is a relatively recent phenomenon. In his book 'The Making of Europe', Robert Bartlett provides ample evidence that, in the 12th and 13th centuries, the authorities went out of their way to protect minority rights and privileges. In the outer reaches of an expanding Europe, land acquisition and trading brought with them an intermingling of the races, as in Spain, the Slav lands and the Baltic. In many cases, minorities even enjoyed the protection of their native judicial systems.

Although the laws of the time were not always very even-handed in their treatment of ethnic groups - particularly in the Anglo-Norman dominions of Ireland where the natives were treated as an inferior species - the problems we see today would have been unthinkable in the Europe of the Early

Middle Ages. The emergence of the nation-state was the catalyst for a new and harsher view of the status of minorities.

Take a look at the history of Europe and you will see that the happiest and best integrated communities were the urbanised multicultural ones - until the most recent and vindictive form of nationalism emerged in the 20th century. Examples are legion: Viborg in what used to be Finnish Karelia, Liverpool as it used to be, Hanseatic Hamburg, Barcelona with its long and vibrant history, the Genoa of Columbus, Odessa at the time of the Tsars.

The sad truth is that the further one goes into the interior of most European countries, the further one gets away from the spirit of pluralism. At the time of the Maastricht Treaty referendum, it was those areas of so-called 'Republican France' in the centre of the country that were the most resistant to the idea of European unity. It was the communities around the periphery of this nation-state *par excellence*, both on the frontiers with Germany and on the Atlantic seaboard, that showed the greatest commitment to the European ideal.

The same can be said about other European countries. Those communities that have the good fortune to be exposed to other cultures are enriched by their experience and, maybe by force of circumstances, learn to draw on the resources of those other cultures. In the meantime the traditional cultures, happily (or unhappily) unmolested at the heart of the country, continue to exercise their preferences and prejudices, and end up the losers.

In the past hundred years, many of the newly created or rediscovered nations of Europe have demonstrated how beastly they can be to people who are perceived as not being 'national' though present on their land: the Czechs to the Sudeten Germans (2.5 million expelled in 1945), the Greeks to the Slav Macedonians and the Turkish minorities in Thrace, the Romanians to their German and Hungarian minorities, the

Italians to the Friulians and, of course, almost everyone to the Jews and Gypsies.

The last-named, a "transnational minority" of several millions with an important presence in both Romania and Hungary, hope to achieve international recognition for their rights. This has become even more urgent with the discrimination shown against these people in central and eastern Europe since the collapse of communism.

Tony Gatlif, a Gypsy filmmaker, says that "every time things go badly, the Gypsies suffer. Eastern Europe has lost its roots, and the Gypsies are again the scapegoats." And he adds: "Among the Gypsies, I have never seen a child badly treated, or taught to hate other people."

Not that long ago a distasteful deal was struck between Germany and Romania, under which the German government paid the Romanian state to take some of this migrant community back. Incidentally the Gypsies - or Rom as they prefer to call themselves - are one of the few ethnic groups never to have gone to war against another people. Some Europeans would of course say they have done worse than that, such is their image as chicken thieves and child snatchers.

Also nomadic and equally concerned about their human rights are the Sami of the Arctic Circle, known to most people as the Lapps. As with the Gypsies no one, least of all the Sami themselves, is absolutely sure of their numbers - the best estimate is 50,000 to 60,000 - but there are communities in Norway, Sweden, Finland and Russia. Curiously, their biggest dispute has been with normally fairminded Sweden, where they have been at issue with the government over land ownership and hunting and fishing rights.

'Privileged immigrant workers'

Despite French ultra-right complaints about the number of English people settling in the Dordogne (and Dutch people

The Story of a Sudetenlander

"My roots did not have favourable conditions for growth. I was born in Sudetenland, in the northern corner of what is now the Czech Republic. As Sudetenland has been eradicated from the map, my existence is founded on the void that it left. And yet I want to claim a piece of ground, a cultural heritage for myself.

"The border regions of Czechoslovakia were first settled by German-speaking tribes in the 12th century, and remained Germanic until they were forcibly integrated into Czechoslovakia in 1918. These German-speaking people were part of Hitler's Germany from the time of the Munich convention until 1945. This annexation meant my father had to fight in Hitler's army. At the end of the war, my family was expelled from Sudetenland to Germany together with three million refugees of German origin.

"In 1946 - I was just over a year old - we were ordered to leave... Like cattle, we were boarded up in wagons bound for an unknown existence... My father had just been released from an American prisoner-of-war camp and was working on a farm in Germany. With luck, stubbornness, diligence and bribery, he had been able to find out about our transport and was waiting for us when we reached Southern Germany after our seven-day odyssey...

"I was eleven when my father found a job in Switzerland. I clearly remember the joy and delight I felt: there are no wars in Switzerland! I could barely believe my good fortune. We had a real apartment with central heating, a bathroom and a toilet all to ourselves! What luxury, what paradise! But then came the first day at school. I had no idea how different Swiss German was from Schwaebisch. The teacher made a joke, the whole class laughed; except me - I had not understood a word. I felt forlorn, cut off. And I sat alone, because 'Germans stank'. Suddenly it was wrong to be German, when in Germany it had been wrong NOT to be German. In history class we drew the battle-field of Morgarten in 1315, but there were no safe versions of the war that had just happened. When I asked my parents, I could feel their scars tearing. I did not want to see my mother cry."

From 'Some Roots Start in Pockets' by Heidrun West ('Cupid's Wild Arrows, Bergli Books Ltd, 1993)

A world without borders...

"What shall I tell my children? What shall I say to my Maria, born in Zagreb but living in Belgrade with her mother who is a Croat and her father who is a Montenegrin? What is she? How should she behave? Whom should she love, and whom hate?

"I will teach her honestly and teach her that a person is a person, regardless of where he was born and where he lives. For me, the world was always without borders. That is why this creation of a tribal community on the threshold of the 21st century is incomprehensible to me.

"I am desperate, in fear, in horror, in the expectation of something still more terrible. I am afraid for my children. I am afraid for their future. Who has the right to deprive them of their childhood? Who has the right to deprive them of a future? Who has the right to wage war in my name?

"We are little people; we desire only our modest life. How many people have lost their lives, families, fathers, husbands, become homeless? How many lives of children have been wrecked? In the name of what?"

Extract from a letter written in 1991 by a Yugoslav parent to a friend in Tashkent, Uzbekistan settling in the Ardèche), intra-European Union minorities are rarely a problem today. The only real issue seems to be the proclivity of wealthy Germans for acquiring property on their neighbours' land, in particular Denmark and Austria.

Of the 370 million inhabitants of the European Union, only five million live outside their home-country and even less - 3.1 million - actually work in another member state. Many of these belong to the group classed by sociologists as 'privileged immigrant workers', where the word 'worker' is a bit of a misnomer. The manual workers of the inter-war 30s and post-war 50-60s - largely Italians, Portuguese and Poles - have long since been assimilated.

It is the immigrant minorities from outside the EU that constitute the problem today, partly because they they seem and are different, and partly because they provide a useful scapegoat for the more unscrupulous elements in society, leaders or followers.

Immigrant minorities are even a problem in well-meaning societies like the United States, where naturally decent and democratic instincts are institutionalised and sometimes deformed into affirmative action, political correctness, and the like. Here again, immigrants often stand in as scapegoats for the failures of the politico-economic policies of government. In short, minorities are a nuisance, but a useful one.

Yet if we take a microscope to the body politic, we see that almost all so-called nations are composed of agglomerations of minorities. At the molecular level, society is composed of idiosyncratic human beings, each of them a minority of one.

It turns out that even a country like Norway, which is thought by foreigners to be homogeneous, has masses of 'minorities', with patterns of speech and behaviour changing from fjord to fjord. In varying degrees this reality applies to every country in Europe, Hungary included, despite all the indications to the contrary.

When we are aware of minorities - and there are many that we are not even aware of - they only exist because they are 'in opposition'. It is a question of relative numbers. With a slight difference in skin, custom or culture, and the help of the 'Us & Them' factor, they are self-defining.

The reasonable way to rid ourselves of minorities is not by ghetto-building or genocide, it is by abandoning this principle of relativity and thereby refusing to treat them as such. But, to do that, we need the incentive of a different social organisation, a redeployment of Europe with the aim of enlarging the frame of reference or having no frame at all.

One step has been taken with the creation of the European Union, although some member states are still reluctant to confront their minority problems. The ultimate step is to cease thinking in 'Us & Them' terms, and let time and tolerance do the trick. The alternative of reorganising Europe as a series of culturo-genetic ghettos is no solution at all.

One of the few European countries with a relatively clear conscience in respect of its treatment of minorities is the Netherlands which has, in the words of an American observer, "a national commitment to pluriformality". The one major lapse, its treatment of the Moluccans, seems to have reinforced its commitment.

The Swedes, as well as their Nordic neighbours, have also tried hard to accommodate their new minorities: every immigrant is entitled to instruction in his or her mother-tongue, at great cost to the state. But, like most western nations, they find the process of assimilation increasingly difficult in these recessionary times.

The Austrians have been exemplary in their protection of their Slovene minority, possibly egged on by fears of a repetition of the failed *putsch* of 1923.

Politically even Switzerland has minorities, three of them - the French-speaking community on the other side of the *Röstigraben* in the *Suisse Romande*, the Italian speakers of the Ticino, and the Italian-speaking and Rhaeto-Romansch-speaking inhabitants of the eastern cantons. Yet in reality there are a lot more, since every canton has its own identity and almost every valley of German Switzerland has a dialect and a subculture of its own.

Renowned for their intolerance of anything that deviates from the norm, the Swiss voted emphatically in March 1996 to give 'semi-official' status to their minority language, Rhaeto-Romansch, even though it is spoken by less than one per cent of the Swiss population. More significantly, they have been much more generous than most of their neighbours in accepting refugees from Yugoslavia, surprisingly so in view of their earlier record on immigrants.

Alto Adige and Ostkantone

The Italians, despite the power nexus in Rome, have shown great astuteness in their handling of linguistic issues in the Alto Adige, prior to 1919 the Südtirol region of the Austro-Hungarian empire. Nearly two-thirds of the province's inhabitants are German-speaking, with an additional 20,000 speaking Ladino, a related tongue to Switzerland's Rhaeto-Romansch.

In his book 'The New Italians', Charles Richards states that Italy's "solution to the knotty issue of ethnic minority rights is being touted as a model for minorities in the new Europe of the regions, of a Europe without national or state boundaries".

Italian policy on language learning in Alto Adige has been more respectful of minority rights than of the need to integrate the original populations with the Italian 'settlers' moved in by Mussolini. Yet in the recent elections the people of the province, regardless of origin, showed themselves readier to align with the Lega Nord against Rome than to perpetuate their domestic squabbles.

Charles Richards illustrates the confusions of identity such situations create: "I met younger natives of Bolzano whose parents had come from Naples and Calabria, and they simply defined themselves as Italians, from Alto Adige. Ask liberal German-speakers today how they view themselves, and they will probably respond that they are Italians of German mother tongue. Many, however, prefer to call themselves simply 'Europeans'. Calling themselves European obviates any need to define themselves narrowly as in one community or another. It is an understandable emotional and intellectual position. But it is not acceptable within the law. For the laws in Alto Adige (Südtirol) require one to be either German-speaking or Italian-speaking. There are no half-measures." So much for mixed marriages.

Belgium, the scene of a polarised standoff between Flemings and Walloons, also has its language laws as well as an often overlooked minority, the German speakers of the *Ostkantone*. The history of this small community is an object-lesson in its own right on the nonsense of nationalism. It also shows how the sins(?) of the fathers are visited on... the grandchildren.

The *Ostkantone* had been incorporated into the new state of Prussia at the Congress of Vienna in 1815. With the creation in 1830 of the Kingdom of Belgium - which, many people would say, was a mistake in itself - Brussels' mistrust of Prussia added fuel to the newly kindled fire of Belgian nationalism.

At the end of WWI a Belgian faction, led by the historian and political activist Baron Nothomb, lobbied furiously for the concept of a 'Greater Belgium' to stretch eastwards to the left bank of the Rhine!

Germany having come out the loser, the Belgian government attempted to exercise its right as a surrogate victor. But, far from reaching the left bank of the Rhine, Belgium ended up settling for an area of upland country, essentially given over to farming and forestry, with a population of German-speakers that today numbers some 68,000 souls.

These Frankish people, who had originally settled in the region in the 6th century AD, had been pushed around by whatever Powers-That-Be happened to be around at the time - ending up, in rapid succession, as citizens of Prussia, then the German Empire, then Belgium.

Today, their descendants are the most nationally conscious of all the people of the Kingdom of Belgium. The younger generations cling to their identity as Belgians where their Flemish and Walloon counterparts tend to shrug at the idea.

This difference in attitude is generated, ironically, by a nationalist-inspired act of vindictiveness at the end of WWII, when the Belgian authorities withdrew the civil rights of all those who had continued to work under the Nazi occupation as schoolteachers, hospital administrators and public servants.

This crass treatment, not surprisingly, had a profound effect on the families of the people concerned. They had reason to bear a grudge against the Belgian state.

More surprisingly, the event has since produced generations that, far from feeling any resentment, are now distancing themselves as much as possible from the *German* culture. In the circumstances, the only way out is to be 'Belgian'.

When Edward Mortimer of the *Financial Times* asked one of them what he would do in the event of the breakup of Belgium, he replied: "We are the only real Belgians... If Belgium breaks up, we'll probably ask to join Luxembourg".

It seems that, as 'Belgians' at least, the people of the *Ostkantone* are the majority!

An extreme case

To appreciate the proportions of the minority problem, take a look at the countries further to the east.

The dissolution of the USSR in 1991, and the ethnic and social turmoil that followed, led to the progressive displacement of no less than nine million people. Altogether some 23 million ethnic Russians ended up, high and dry, outside their home country. There were smaller but equally significant upheavals in central and eastern Europe.

Today, Russians are stranded in the Central Asian republics and the Baltic States, Poles in Lithuania, Germans and Ukrainians in Poland, Romanians in Moldova, Serbs in Croatia and Slovenia, and so on. Some of them have been where they are for a very long time.

The Iron Curtain collapsed to reveal more than two million ethnic Germans within the confines of the Soviet Union. The million or so Volga Germans had arrived there over 200 years before, at the invitation of Catherine the Great, but were uprooted and removed by Stalin to Kazakhstan in WWII.

Since the late-1980s, more than a million of these and other ethnic Germans have returned to the mother-country with full citizens' rights. But there are obviously still a lot of people claiming German blood in the ex-USSR - so many that the mother-country has now decided to reduce the annual immigrant quota to 220,000.

Three million Hungarians, a relatively distinctive stock, live as minorities in four neighbouring countries: Slovakia, Romania, the Yugoslav province of Vojvodina (the scene of an experiment in multi-ethnic living under the Habsburgs), and western Ukraine. There are also a lot of them in the US

The Greek psyche, laden with myths, is outperformed by the Cypriots who seem to have no respect for reality at all. This is well illustrated in the conversation held by Sir Walter Bodmer with two Cypriot Orthodox monks (see page ??).

Not long ago an international newspaper referred to the "Turkish "invasion of Cyprus" in 1974. This produced a couple of letters to the editor, one from a Turkish Cypriot, the other from a Greek Cypriot.

The Turkish Cypriot said: "This statement is one-sided and incorrect. Turkey intervened, after a coup by those seeking union with Greece, to save the Turkish Cypriot community from a massacre that had already started."

The Greek Cypriot said: "Although the United Nations knows very well that Turkey invaded Cyprus in 1974, it continues to view the tension there as a dispute between two communities, the Greek Cypriots and the Turkish Cypriots. This is an outrage. The Turks occupy a third of Cyprus, have imported settlers to take over land once held by Greeks and have created a Turkish state recognized only by Turkey."

Two ways of looking at the same problem. As Sir Walter found out, the peoples are one and the same. Which only goes to prove that culture, particularly when its origins go back into the mists of history, is the real culprit, whether that culture expresses itself through language, religion, food or whatever. So ultimately it is Man himself who is to blame. We are collectively duped by our collective unconscious.

city of Cleveland. In fact one-third of all Hungarians now live outside the mother-country.

Of course the ones in Cleveland moved there relatively recently. But it would be wrong to think that the minorities issue is a 19th or even a 20th century phenomenon. The Magyars have been in the Transylvania region of what is now Romania since the 9th century, the Szekely family of Magyars since the 11th century, and the Saxons since the mid-12th century.

Another way of illustrating the minority problem is to take the case of Vojvodina, admittedly an extreme case thanks to a well-intentioned but perhaps ill-advised initiative by the Habsburg monarchs.

According to a Yugoslav researcher, Vesna Marjanovic, the province can now claim more than 15 minorities alongside the Serb majority of 1,131,000 (1991 figures, rounded off). These include 341,000 Hungarians, 74,000 Croats, 64,000 Slovaks, 39,000 Romanians, 20,000 Gypsies, 18,000 Rutains, 10,000 Bunjevci, 2,500 Bulgarians, 2,000 Czechs, 200 Sokci and handsful of Poles, *Volksdeutsche* and Kliments from Albania!

In the meantime, a bloody internecine fight has led to a carve-up of Bosnia between an 'ethnically pure' community of Serbs and a bizarre condominium of Croats and Bosnian Muslims. Their neighbours are now an almost Serb-less Croatia and a more or less Croat-less Serbia, Vojvodina excepted. They, and we, look like ending up with a series of ghettos. What kind of a Europe is that?

Thinking of which, on the basis of bloodcount alone, Kosovo should be handed over to the Albanians. As for Albania, since 1991 an estimated half-million young people - one-sixth of the entire population - have left the country to find a better living elsewhere.

Even a relatively 'unbalkanised' situation like Mostar, with only Croats and Muslims involved, proved too much for the town's first EU administrator, Hans Koschnick, who bravely risked his reputation on the creation of a mixed district in the centre of the city - and then resigned. With the benefit of hindsight his successor, Richard Casado, was able to point out that "you cannot unite people by decree".

The Romanian government, no better than its communist predecessors, has an overtly discrimatory policy towards the country's minorities, Hungarian and German-speaking. In fact the latter is no longer a great problem since, of the 800,000 German speakers in the Siebenburgen area at the beginning of WWII, all but 90,000 have since returned to Germany under the *Volksdeutsche* regime or are dead.

When all is said and done, minority attitudes can be just as pernicious as majority ones. Whereas majorities tend to impose their status unthinkingly, there is a conscious minority mentality which amounts to a *reductio ad absurdum*.

It is best expressed in the words of a North African tribesman: "I defend my country against other countries, I defend my region against my country, I defend my town against the region, I defend my tribe against the town, I defend my family against the tribe, and I defend my brother against the family."

That, surely, is no solution either.

The Birth of
New Nations?

"People like myself see regionalism - or even, as in our specific Catalan case, non-secessionist nationalism - as above all else an act of affirmation of one's own identity; the cultural fact has primordial importance"

Jordi Pujol, President of the Autonomous Government of Catalonia

"I believe in the virtue of small nations"

André Gide

"At first glance, it seems ironic that European countries are splitting at the seams just as they gear up for the first continent-wide federation they've ever seen"

Stephen D Jones, '*Unity and Disunity in the New Europe'*

"The Welsh, Irish and Scottish have all effectively been annexed by the English and seen their languages eroded almost to vanishing point"

Peter Millar, *The Sunday Times*

"There, as in the stateless nations of Catalonia and Scotland, we are witnessing nation-building of a new sort, one that recognises the limitations of statehood and sovereignty and is more in tune with the realities of the modern world than are the defenders of the old state order"

Michael Keating, University of Western Ontario

"What the French don't understand is that this is a people with their own identity. What irritates people here is the persistent refusal of the authorities in Paris to recognise this identity" **Noëlle Vincensini, *Corsican intellectual***

Some western European countries, out of mixed motives, have already ventured down the regionalisation road or at least the decentralisation of certain powers.

Switzerland got off to an early start, egged on in the year 1515 by the battle of Marignano, which the Swiss lost. As a result the Swiss cantons existed as sovereign states long before the enactment of a federal constitution in 1848. They are not simply administrative areas, but independent small states with their own political institutions.

For the Swiss, federalism is a fact of life, subtly balancing the distribution of state authority between the cantons and the Confederation. Even if outside observers find the Swiss way of life somewhat forbidding, the country deserves credit for its efforts to ensure multilingual and multicultural co-existence. Maybe, after all, Switzerland could serve as a model for the Europe of the future?

Neighbouring Austria, straddled between an empire and oblivion, also opted for decentralisation of authority in its new constitution as a republic. Substantial powers were given to its nine provinces, with its local assemblies represented in the national upper house, the *Bundesrat*.

Even centralist France, abandoning its Jacobin principles for once, devolved some of its powers to the provinces during the Mitterand presidency.

But the most radical 'regionaliser' in post-war western Europe has been West Germany, as it used to be called, though only partially prompted by its own convictions. It was the victorious Allies who imposed a federal structure on the country - ironically with the intention of weakening German political power for once and for all!

Prime movers in this initiative were the British and the French. According to that most statesmanlike of presidents, Richard von Weizsäcker, the British - fervent believers in the 'first past the post' system - gave Germany proportional representation. The French, an almost neurotically centralist society, gave the Germans federalism. Both nations, thinking they were acting in their own best interests, put Germany in a situation that was to have historic and, for the victim, very positive consequences.

Moreover the emerging political classes in Germany accepted the need to create a system which distanced itself from previous regimes and, at the same time, created a series of bulkheads to stem any obsessive power-mongering from the centre.

Unsurprisingly, the Bavarians at first rejected the new constitution and contemplated complete independence or union with Austria (a curious parallel with Austria's Vorarlberg province, which voted after WWI to merge with neighbouring Switzerland, only to be turned down flatly by the Swiss!).

The German federal constitution of 1949 set out "to create *Länder* which by their size and capacity are able to fulfil the functions incumbent upon them". Today's 16 *Länder* have extensive powers of their own, but are bound through a system called *Finanzausgleich* to provide financial support to those *Länder* in need.

The German spirit of solidarity, though severely strained by the reunification process, is still evident. However, one instance where German solidarity failed to pass the test was the proposed amalgalmation of Berlin and Brandenburg as part of a plan to reduce the 16 *Länder* to eight jumbo-states. Brandenburgers were evidently disinclined to bail out near-bankrupt Berlin.

Another country, acting out of equally grassroots motives, is newly federalised Belgium which currently comprises three regions - Flanders, the so-called French Community and the Brussels Region, as well as the German-speaking community of the *Ostkantone* (the irredentist Flemish hope to eliminate Brussels as a separate region in due course). Here 'desolidarisation' is the password.

Belgium is, of course, an accident of other people's history, which partly explains why the Belgian situation is such a complex one. The country was cobbled together in 1830 by the Great-Powers-That-Were and had a small bit of Greater Germany stitched on to it in 1918. What emerged was a sort of a nation which, despite a considerable yet rarely acknowledged degree of ethnic homogeneity - as far as anyone can tell, they are essentially Salian Franks with an admixture of Celtic - had not so much else in common.

While parts of what is now called Wallonia had thrived in the early Middle Ages, much of Flanders was still a peasant community. When Flemish culture - led by Bruges, Ghent and Antwerp - bloomed in the 14th century, Walloon culture had difficulty in competing. In fact the Flemish culture, misleadingly called 'Burgundian' from the ruling dynasty of the time, had few rivals in Europe. But Flemish cultural distinction, its fortunes linked closely to the prosperity of the wool industry, subsequently waned.

With the arrival of the Industrial Revolution, Wallonia used its natural resources to get the upper hand economically. Brussels had seen the emergence of an elitist French-speaking bourgeoisie which, both through its acts and its unspoken attitudes, treated the Flemish community as second-class citizens.

Many of the poorer but industrious members of the Flemish community, particularly those from the outlying agricultural communities of Flanders, moved into Brussels as tradespeople. They abandoned the Flemish language in favour of French, and eventually became more rabid in their disdain of their own people than the French-speakers were.

Letter to the editor of 'The European' newspaper (29.11.1995)

"I cannot agree with certain MEPs who want to ignore the agreement of the 1992 Edinburgh summit to hold 12 sessions in Strasbourg. Actually, this is a new attempt to bring the European Parliament over to Brussels, and thus add to the already overpowering bureaucracy of Brussels. This would worsen the situation of the people in the Belgian capital, who have to endure the consequences of the urban, social and, in the case of Dutch-speakers in Brussels[1], cultural disaster brought about by the Europeanisation of a medium-sized city.

Since a 1970 census more than 300,000 Brusselers[2] of Belgian nationality have had to quit their city under this strain. We believe European institutions should decentralise in order to cut back the great cost of maintaining bases in three cities[3]. Strasbourg might as well be the sole seat of the European Parliament[4].

We believe that Europe should become a large and free confederation of states, whose essential function would be to guarantee free movement of products, people, ideas and capital within the framework of some sort of an improved EFTA[5]. Such a Europe would be more in the spirit of the fathers of the Treaty of Rome than the centralised federal state which the Maastricht Treaty implies[6].

(signed)

André Monteyne[7], President,
Flemish Committee for Brussels
Belgium"

---

1. Here we're getting to the real point. The writer and others of his ilk want to get Brussels back to what it used to be, a largely Flemish (-speaking) city, regardless of the realities of the late-20th century.

2. Note the choice of word. There is no evidence of whom they are or why they left. The process of inner-city emigration towards the suburbs is universal.

3. 'Decentralise' implies locating in even more cities, hence even greater cost and not the opposite!

4. Why pass the baby to poor little ol' Strasbourg, which is a quarter the size of Brussels? In any case, the 'Brusselers' want to get as many institutions as possible - they know well enough which side their bread is buttered on - even if Strasbourg is determined to go through hell and high water to keep the European Parliament.

5. Apart from the minimalist thinking, who's going to believe that the writer really believes in 'the free movement of people and ideas' at the European level, when he's contributing to the creation of a ghetto mentality at home?

6. Would it? I wonder.

7. French-sounding name, acute accent and all...

These developments produced an understandable reaction on the Flemish side. They reasserted their identity on the basis of their long-standing culture and the new 19th-century ideology of linguistic and cultural uniqueness, overriding all evidence of their ethnic relationship to other Belgians.

Eric Hobsbawm, in his book 'Nations and Nationhood since 1780', describes the dilemma: "The new Flemish-educated class found itself poised between the Flemish masses, whose most dynamic elements were drawn to French because of the practical advantages of knowing that language, and the upper levels of the Belgian administration, culture and affairs, which remained unshakeably francophone."

The separate destinies of the two main communities in Belgium had become enmeshed in linguistic and class differences to produce an almost impenetrable web of misconceptions, myths and ultimately mistrust.

Bring on the politicians (and, to a lesser degree, the Catholic church) who made, and are still making, merry hell of the situation - not exactly to their credit, in the view of many sensible Belgians - and the whole thing gets out of hand.

The prize for narrow-mindedness

Today, the tables have been turned and Flanders is again in the ascendency. Belgian community politics has now reached the state that, to an outsider, it is bizarre to the point of being positively kafkaesque. An example, intentional or otherwise, of the bad faith of the political classes is provided by the letter reproduced on the preceding page.

It has to be said, though, that the prize for narrow-mindedness, if not political demagoguery, goes without question to the current minister-president of Flanders. He rightly interprets democracy as "getting closer to the people", but then goes on to use this as a justification for getting further away from the people he *doesn't* represent.

Real democracy starts with human rights *per se*. But then, for different reasons, the president of the French-language community is no better.

The fact of setting one group of people against another, albeit in the process of redressing historical injustices, may ultimately rebound to the detriment of the politicians concerned - particularly if the younger generation of Belgians shares, with its contemporaries, the kind of attitudes expressed in chapter 8. The Flemish government seems to be pointing in the opposite direction to the one now being taken by most of Europe's educated young people.

Depending on their position in the political spectrum, the Flemish parties offer qualified support for the existing federal union or clamour for total separation, presumably in the context of something bigger. The most that can be hoped for at the time of writing could be called 'conditional solidarity', i.e. a solidarity which is conditional on the mutual benefits for all involved.

With the present sorry state of key parts of the Walloon economy - and the cost of unemployment pay and social services, to which the Flemish feel they are contributing unduly - this interpretation of 'solidarity' sounds more like self-interest. If federalism is to extend more widely across Europe, we will have to do better than that.

It is of course neither appropriate not convenient to point to the genetic homogeneity of Belgians, Flemish and Walloons, not just in terms of their origins, but also because of the constant intermarriage and miscegenation in the centuries since. Simple evidence of this is the number of Flemish people with French-sounding names and vice versa.

Nor, though they are proud of it, do the Belgians particularly want to be reminded of another thing they have in common, namely their 'Burgundian' culture. Yet sociologists and others note that there is no greater difference between two neighbouring European cultures than between Belgium, all of it, and the Netherlands. Which is another way of saying, as many people have said, that the Belgians do indeed have a lot in common.

When all is said and done, Flemish nationalism - or whatever you want to call it - is a hangover from the days when the French-language elite in Belgium discriminated against the Flemish. This is not that long ago. In fact there are French speakers I know who still practice it subconsciously.

Yet the syndrome is essentially a hangover and, like all hangovers, the best thing the sufferer can do is get rid of it as quickly as possible. Do the Flemish want to end up in a ghetto of their own making? They are even now doing their best to isolate that multicultural community *par excellence,* Brussels, with sinister symbolical acts like a bicycle marathon around the Flemish perimeter of the capital city - an event that

Flemish kids are encouraged to participate in, in full knowledge of what it implies.

Even more sinister is a recent action plan to reinforce the application of the language laws in the peripheral communes of Brussels. This includes, amongst other monstrosities, provision for regional and provincial inspectors to ensure the use of Dutch in official communal and intercommunal proceedings. Language Police now, Thought Police next?

Unfortunately such behaviour is encouraging the Walloons to practice a similarly morbid form of cultural and linguistic nationalism within this oh-so-small country. Spurred on by the Flemish example, some of the more extremist elements in what is erroneously called 'the French Community of Belgium' are even more rabid.

The problem with Belgian inter-community politics - which could show the way to the rest of Europe, but doesn't - is that it is polarised: Flemish against French-speakers, and vice versa (in this case the German-speakers simply don't count). This encourages a manicheistic frame of mind which is notably absent from most other countries experiencing centrifugal trends, in particular Spain.

At the end of the day, one asks oneself why these eminently admirable, decent and sensible people allow themselves to be led astray to the point of accepting different educational systems, two lots of everything (including bureaucrats) and a top-heavy tax system. Maybe it's because they're so good at tax evasion.

Happily, there are more and more Belgians, particularly Flemish, who acknowledge their luck in finding themselves on the great faultline of Europe, the one where the Germanic and the Latin cultures meet. For minds that are open, this is a window onto two different yet closely interrelated worlds.

A 'Europe of the Regions', as posited in the final chapter of this book, would help meet the grievances and aspirations of the Flemish. They might then be encouraged to adopt a more sympathetic attitude towards their Walloon relatives.

They could certainly take a lesson from the older generations of Finns for whom, in the words of historian Matti Klinge, "upward social mobility was impossible without a good command of Swedish". Despite this, the Finnish majority and Swedish minority have since learned to bury the hatchet.

Not quite. There is still a problem below the surface - jealousies that emerge when a Finnish Finn and Swedish Finn vie for the same top job - but at least it is not exploited politically.

"Spain is ahead"

It is significant that the three communities at the front of the field in the race to regionalise - the Flemish, the Catalans and the people of northern Italy - all share a glorious past in European medieval history.

It is also ironic that these communities, which at the time were as open and cosmopolitan as any you could find, are now betraying their traditions by being more inward-turned than most of their neighbours.

Since the Catholic Kings, Spain has been a centralist country, nonetheless gaining strength from its strong regional diversity. There are striking cultural and linguistic differences between the people of central Castile-Leon, the Catalans and the part-Celtic, part-Swabian Galicians for example. The Andalusians have another, distinctive lifestyle. As for the Basques, they are genetically quite distinct, with a very high rhesus negative blood factor.

With this tradition of centralism, it is all the more surprising how smoothly the government of Adolfo Suarez and its successors introduced the principle and apparatus of 17 semi-autonomous *comunidades* or regions from 1978 onwards as part of Spain's transition to post-Franco democracy.

These regions have less devolved power than the German *Länder,* who have been the pacemakers in European regionalisation as in many other things since WWII. But in the opinion of Pasqual Maragall, mayor of Barcelona and president of the EU's Committee of the Regions, "Spain is ahead of many European countries in the decentralisation of government and enfranchisement of its people."

Explaining his personal standpoint, Maragall says: "I'm a militant believer in the cause of politics being essentially a matter of proximity between people and their representatives. The only level that interests me more is politics at the European level."

Jordi Pujol, the Catalan president, believes that proximity of government releases energies that centralised administrations stifle. His judgement is severe: "it is centralism, with its rigidities and restrictions, which is a factor of stagnation."

In the context of a Europe which seems incapable of solving its unemployment problems, he may have a point. Proximity in the form of personal relationships between bosses and workers in the SME sector produces both resilience and reluctance to terminate relationships. There is a will to find a common solution. Maybe the same applies at the level of the region.

Juan Pablo Fusi Aizpurua, history professor at Madrid's Complutense University, asserts on the other hand that Spanish regional policy "is expensive and there is an overlapping of the various administrations". Democracy is achieved with a loss in economies of scale. The cost, according to Spanish sociologist Rafael López Pintor, can be monumental but "this problem is never faced because you cannot put a price on the question of regional identity".

It seems however that, despite the cost, Spain's regions are determined to fight for more autonomy and less dependence on what, 500 years ago, was Europe's centralist state par excellence. Under the clever and ambitious Jordi Pujol, working from a relatively narrow power base, the Catalans have made massive inroads into central government powers.

The price for their support in the Cortes has included not only concessions on job training, police and ports administration, but also the prospect of retaining one-third of income tax revenue within the region, compared with the 15 per cent that applied previously.

Pujol's championship of regional rights has also meant that Spain's 17 autonomous communities will be consulted by government on any issues that affect them directly. They will also, together with the German *Länder* and the two principal Belgian communities, have their representatives on European Union committees and working groups, including in certain circumstances that Holy-of-Holies, the Council of Ministers.

There are also strong chances that the upper house of the Spanish *Cortes* will be remodelled as a chamber representing Spain's regions, along the lines of the *Bundesrat* of Germany and Austria.

One of the staunchest champions of a greater degree of devolvement, leading possibly to Spain's mutation into a federal state, is Manuel Fraga Iribarne, president of Galicia and one of the architects of the 1978 constitutional changes under Adolfo Suarez. In his words, "this is a good moment for those of us who wrote the constitution to use our authority to call for its reform, and argue against those who want it to stay the same."

"Many diverse peoples settled in that part of northeast Spain now known as Catalonia, including Alans, Berbers, Carthaginians and their allies, Celts, Franks, Goths, Greeks, Iberians, Moors, Phoenicians, Romans and their subjects, Vandals and Visigoths. When was it ever a nation?

Catalonia consisted of several Marches, counties and dukedoms which later became part of the Christian kingdom of Aragon. Catalonia has been part of the Carthaginian conquests, part of a Roman province, a part of the Moorish emirates, part of Charlemagne's Frankish empire, part of the kingdom of Aragon, part of France and is now part of Spain.

Not only do the Catalan nationalists appear to be rewriting history - an official publication describes the origin of the nation when 'King' Borrell II broke his ties with France - they are also redrawing the map of Europe. Catalan expansionism extends to the French *département* of Pyrénées Orientales, south and east to the Balearic Islands, Murcia and the Valencian community. They demand that the most productive and fertile areas should be added to the Catalan empire.

Giving way to their demands may buy a few months, or even a couple of years, of stable government. But can Spain afford to pay the price? I think not.

Letter to 'The European' newspaper from a British reader living in Spain.

The Spanish model will certainly benefit from fine-tuning. As a champion of regionalisation, Maragall thinks the formula will flourish. "In the long term, I believe we will have a Europe of the regions and behind that, a Europe of the cities. Europe will be a safer place if it devolves power both to its regions, which means particularity, and its cities, which means proximity and common citizenship."

"We in Catalonia believe we are a distinct nation with our own language, culture and traditions", says Jordi Pujol. "We are not seeking independence, but we want Madrid to recognise our difference and our rights."

An interesting argument when, on the Catalan government's own admission, 40 per cent of the region's population consists of settlers from other parts of Spain and their children!

"Now we must make Italians"

Polled by the newspaper *La Repubblica* in 1993, 18 per cent of respondents said they thought Italy would become a confederation of sovereign regions within ten years, and 26 per cent doubted whether it would still be a single unified country.

They could well be proved right. Italy is a geographically coherent but culturally unrealistic entity that arrived as a backrunner in the race to nation-statehood. Its creation, orchestrated by Count Cavour with Vittorio Emanuele II and Garibaldi in the lead roles, took no account of the different cultures, even ethnic groups, inhabiting the peninsula.

Where the people of the north are largely of Germanic stock (Lombard = 'long beard'), those of the south have Arab and Greek blood in their veins as well as Lombard. The people have little in common except that they all carry Italian passports. As Massimo d'Azeglio, the Piedmontese prime minister, said shortly after unification: "We have created Italy, now we must make the Italians".

At the time the country could not even claim a common language, with people speaking local dialects like Lombard, Occitano, Venetian, Neapolitan, Sicilian, Friulian, even Greek. As a result, Tullio de Mauro estimated that only 2.5 per cent of the population was able to speak Italian as it is understood today!

It was in fact the Sicilians who originally objected most strongly to this cobbling together of a nation-state. Unification came from the top down, the people were not consulted. For people like Lampedusa's hero in 'Il Gattopardo', it was nothing more nor less than an invasion from the north.

Steps were taken to remedy this century-old grievance after WWII. The first move towards the federalisation of Italy came with the regional autonomy legislation of 1946. Sicily was the subject of a special statute which gave the island jurisdiction over its police, town and infrastructure planning, and industrial and agricultural legislation. This suited the Mafia well, with the result that little was done to exercise the prorogatives implicit in Sicily's special constitutional status.

The second step was the division of the country into 20 administrative regions in 1975, followed by two enactments of additional competences for regional administrations. Now the Italian islands - Capri, Elba, Ponza, Ischia, Lipari, Pantelleria and Lampedusa - are lobbying for a 21st region.

Feeling itself at least partially liberated from the incubus of the Mafia, Sicily is starting to reassert its status with claims to an even greater degree of self-determination. But the strongest challenge to the state now comes from the north itself, championed by the Lega Nord and its allies.

Resentment over the mismanagement of a corrupt political class - associated in peoples' minds essentially with Rome, to the south - is exacerbated by the feeling that northerners' money is being poured indiscriminately into the deep south, Sicily and the Mezzogiorno.

In the words of Umbert Bossi, the populist leader of the Lega Nord party, "there are two economies, north and south, and so there should be two treasuries and two central banks". In short, like Ms Thatcher, he wants his money back. They already have a name for their new statelet, Padania, which sounds like a brand of coffee. They also have their own legislature and plans for a currency.

The revamped Lega Nord is uncompromising now in its demands for nothing less than the federalisation of Italy, with a north-south partition as its ultimate goal. Its ill-advised electoral pact with Silvio Berlusconi's Forza Italia and the Allianza Nazionale stood in the way in 1994.

"We found all roads to federalism blocked", says Giancarlo Pagliarini, Bossi's associate and now self-styled prime minister of Italy's 'government of the north'. "We learned that change via Rome was useless."

"There is an enormous energy in young Italians which remains untapped", comments an Italian official, himself in his early 30s. "They are demoralised because they see no openings for their creativity in the country as it is. So they have opted out."

"What Judge Di Pietro needed to do was clean up the whole system - he didn't go far enough. All the parties, even the communists, were recruiting the wrong people, the ones ready to compromise, to play tricks, to do anything necessary to ensure the survival of their party. The best people in Italy are not in politics, they are in industry and in the private sector." Judge Di Pietro is now Italy's Minister of Public Works!

Despite his insistence that "Italy's unity is not open for discussion", newly elected Prime Minister Romano Prodi immediately promised constitutional change with a strong dose of federalism. One can only hope that this political process will take full account of the cultural realities - and that at the same time what sense of solidarity is left among Italians will survive. Remember the Extended Family?

Even someone as traditionalist as Giovanni Agnelli, the recently retired head of FIAT, states flatly that within the context of the Italian state he would like to see Piedmont with the same powers as Bavaria.

In his book 'The New Italians', British journalist and writer Charles Richards looks at the reasons for the decline of a national identity such as it was and, as a felicitous side-effect, young Italians' particularly strong attachment to the European ideal. Two factors are the relatively short history of the Italian nation-state and the fact that the country was on the losing side in WWII.

But, he continues, "the weakness of the state may not be reason enough for the decline in a sense of identity, but it is a contributory cause. Some historians have also attributed a diminished sense of the state to the overriding power and influence of the political parties, which demanded loyalties and ties over and above any elsewhere accorded to the state. The weakness of the institutions also undermined any respect for the state." Sounds familiar.

There are still some Italians around who cling to a national identity closely linked to real estate. The issue is Istria, a strategic point at the head of the Adriatic and the crossroads for many nationalist, even imperial, ventures involving Romans, Venetians, French, Austro-Hungarians, Croatians, Slovenes and of course Italians.

All very well - Italy did in fact occupy the peninsula from 1919 to 1945 - but listen to Giuseppe Rota, the principal of an

118

Italian primary school in Umag, now part of Croatia, talking to the 'International Herald Tribune': "Every time there are elections in Italy, they talk about Istria and changing the border and the Osimo Treaty. But changing the border today? What does that mean? Another war, and we are tired of war."

Happily, in the words of the political philosopher Norberto Bobbio, "Italy is no longer a nation in the sense that in the new generation there no longer exists a national sentiment. Italy has become little more than a geographical expression and the Italians are once more becoming a common mass with no name".

"For me", says Giancarlo Pagliarini with the requisite dose of Italian (or should I say 'Padanian'?) hyperbole, "a man or woman from Sicily, Catalonia or Essex are the same. We feel we are a member of Europe much more than a member of Italy". I wonder if Essex Man or Woman feels the same?

Most young Italians today would wholeheartedly agree with Bobbio, if not with Pagliarini. The only question that remains is whether Italy decentralises further, is transformed into a fully federalised state, or simply ceases to exist.

Covering a "meeting on nationalities" in August 1991 in Geneva - the sort of place they have conferences like this - the *Wall Street Journal Europe* met a Mr Alfred Symank, "chief lobbyist of the Sorbian Nationality for Autonomous Lusitania". The significance of 'autonomous' is immediate, it's the 'Lusitania' bit that puzzles. Apparently it's somewhere in what was east Germany.

The event prompted the paper to say the following: "Here is the worst nightmare of every European country with at least one minority aspiring to sovereignty. There are the Serbs in Croatia, the Albanians in Serbia, and the Macedonians in Yugoslavia, Greece and Bulgaria. There are the Georgians and the Crimean Tartars. There are Gypsies, Sorbs and Transylvanians. The Czechs are here, and the Slovaks, too. There are the Finnish-speaking minority in Sweden, the Bretons in France, and the Kurds of Turkey and Iran. The Corsicans would have come, except that they were too busy raising an army to fight for independence from France."

God bless Europe. If she can survive this kind of thing, she can survive anything. Provided, with birthrates plummeting, she can remember how to reproduce herself...

Scepticism
and the State

"One of the chief ironies of the end of the 20th century is that, as democracy takes new root in many parts of the ex-communist world and elsewhere, a growing number of ordinary voters in the older democracies of Europe and North America seem to be increasingly disenchanted with the way their political systems work"

'The Economist', 14/10/1995

"Both fascism and communism emerged in Europe because liberal democracy had failed to live up to its expectations. If it fails again, we may expect new and similar challenges, both in our own continent and throughout the world"

Professor Sir Michael Howard, British historian

"Politics are in turmoil. People are no longer content with the limitations of representative democracy. Their model is not the British House of Commons as prevailing power centre but the Swiss referendum"

Guido Brunner, ex-Member of the European Commission

"Political success may well go to those who sound least like politicians"

Douglas Hurd, former British foreign secretary

"In the West, we are more likely to find men and women to admire among environmentalists, feminists, religious leaders, civil-rights activists, and so on, than among politicians of any sort"

Michael Walzer, Princeton Institute for Advanced Study

"The concept of the nation-state shakes hands with the concept of government by consent"

'The Economist', 5/1/1996

If the foregoing chapters have failed to convince of the idiocy of the way we Europeans run our world - and the perils inherent in confronting a completely new global order with the apparatus of the past - then consider the fault-line that is developing within European society itself.

So far we have been talking about the so-to-speak 'vertical' dotted lines that divide European societies from one another. Now, we come to a 'horizontal' dotted line, a major one, which divides most of these societies of western Europe into two.

In the last three years I have talked to over 5,000 people of most European nationalities about their views on contemporary society and the mechanisms of government. Many of these are university graduates or post-graduates in the age-range 18-30. Many of them are beneficiaries of the EU's Erasmus programme, now called Socrates, and convinced Europeans.

Many of them are also, sadly, educated for jobs they cannot find: at the end of 1994 no less than 53 per cent of Spanish under-20s were without work. Yet, from my personal observations, disaffection with the political classes goes much deeper than the dole queue.

Others are middle-aged people taking recycling or continuing-education courses in order to make them fit for reentry into working life. Often, with no alternative, they will end up self-employed. At least, they will have acquired some skills that may serve them well under the new rules of survival.

From my discussions with these groups I find that, with few exceptions, they feel at best disenchantment, at worst disgust, at the way their societies are being run. In the circumstances, it is hardly surprising that they put the blame, without qualification, on their political leaders.

These feelings are most evident in the 18-30 age group, though it is also there in the disaffected middle-aged. The young feel little less than contempt for their political classes. It is an almost unanimous attitude in Belgium, Britain, France, Italy and Spain.

What I would not have expected is that it is also present in Sweden and Finland, countries with a strong democratic tradition and a relatively responsible political class. The only country which emerges relatively unscathed is the Netherlands.

What is even more worrying, though, is that this contempt is accompanied by a very *conscious* state of apathy, even anomie - what might be called symptoms of terminal alienation. The general reaction of young people today is to distance themselves entirely from the world of politics, simply to want nothing to do with it.

The idea of being active politically never occurs to them. They don't even feel inclined to demonstrate their dissatisfaction. For them this is a waste of time. They only protest when their direct interests are affected. In most cases they ask themselves, "what's the point?".

Many of them don't even want to exercise the right to vote. "You can't resolve young people's frustration with politics just by asking them to cast their vote once every five years", says German youth organiser Matthias Baumann.

It can of course be argued that this alienation extends beyond politics into attitudes towards society generally. Even a historically conformist community like Germany now witnesses its own version of 'Generation X' where different tribes of youngsters go their separate ways.

In a poll in early-1996 of over 1,000 German 15-25 year olds, *Stern* magazine was able to identify no less than 21 in-groups ranging from Greens, Jesus Freaks and Computer

Kids to Punks, Girlies and Hillbillies. The keyword, common to all these groups, is 'cool', implying an inclination and ability to take things as they come.

The 1995 edition of the IBM German Youth Study, commissioned from the *Institut für Empirische Psychologie*, found that more than half of the nearly 2,500 respondents, aged 14-24, showed little or no interest in politics, even though 64 per cent of them felt it was important to vote (perhaps reflecting the stronger social conscience of the Germans). The study concluded that "politicians and political parties have an emphatically poor reputation with young people".

"A sense of powerlessness"

These German findings are echoed in the conclusions of a number of recent attitude studies amongst young Europeans of all socio-economic and educational levels.

Already in 1993 the evidence was there. That year the French Publicis group, in association with the AIESEC international student organisation, sponsored a study of over 4,000 undergraduates and business school students from the twelve countries of the European Community, as it was called then. This showed that, where two undergraduates out of three were ready to accept the word of a scientist, only one out of ten was prepared to accept the word of a politician.

Specifically, 81 per cent of those questioned found their politicians devoid of interest, 61 per cent felt they were incompetent (with a slightly lower rate of assent in France, Portugal and Denmark), 85 per cent felt that they didn't take young people into account in their decisions, and 61 per cent thought they were corrupt.

In 1994 Yankelovich Partners, an international market research organisation, made a substantive and detailed study of the attitudes and priorities of over 3,000 young Europeans in the 16-24 and 25-34 age groups (the MTV Europe/ Yankelovich Young Adult Europe MONITOR™).

Individual interviews, of up to one hour in length, were conducted with 500 respondents in each of seven European countries - the United Kingdom, Germany, France, Italy, Spain, Belgium and The Netherlands - plus a further 250 interviews in Sweden.

Of the total of 3,278 valid responses, only 645 or 20 per cent of these young people claimed to be "interested in politics". The highest percentages were in the Netherlands and Sweden (28 per cent and 24 per cent respectively), the lowest the UK (13 per cent) and Belgium (7 per cent). In all cases, the females of the nationality expressed less interest than the males.

Asked whether or not they agreed with the statement that "you used to be able to believe what people in authority told you, but that's not as true as it was", 84 per cent of British respondents concurred, together with 83 per cent of the Dutch and 80 per cent of the Belgians. The Germans, at 66 per cent, were the ones who agreed least.

Further evidence of disengagement comes from the latest edition (1995) of the Research International Observer, a continuing annual examination of young peoples' attitudes and preferences. This programme comprises both group discussions (an average of four groups per country) and interviews with professionals in the 'young adult' sector (average eight per country). The countries covered included all of the European Union member states with the exception of Austria, Ireland and Luxembourg. Findings were analysed in terms of two age groups, 20-25 and 26-35.

The RIO research found "a sense of powerlessness at the individual's ability to influence anything (society, politics, the environment, world issues) at a broader level".

The researchers noted an erosion of the credibility of the system and, by implication, of the political classes in every country they studied. In the UK, they went so far as to record "a strong sense of living in a disfunctional society", which translates into "political apathy, complacency and rationalisation of their impotence".

German youth, according to the RIO researchers, are confronted with "a political landscape which they regard as confusing, complex and very difficult to identify with". Young Italians, understandably in view of recent events, have "a widespread feeling of disorientation. They no longer have any faith in institutions, politics has become something dirty by definition".

Left with a motivational gap after the political ferment of the 1970s, they find that none of the traditional 'producers' of ideals - the church, the political parties, socio-cultural movements - are able to offer replacement ideologies. "There seems to be the conviction", the report concludes, "that the world is mechanically regulated by power relationships".

Young Greeks, says the RIO report, see the world as "a highly demanding, competitive, materialistic and, according to many, superficial and corrupted place". Even in the Netherlands young adults "display 'active resignation' rather than obviously positive or negative attitudes".

A fourth survey by the INRA research group, also undertaken in 1995, showed that scepticism about government extends to other age groups too. This study, which worked on a sample of 18,000 Europeans of 15 years and upwards, found that people in many western European countries, though not all, would like to see the role of government reduced.

Reflecting the all-pervasive nature of the Swedish welfare state, no less than 59.4 per cent of Swedes think it would be a "good thing" if government played a smaller role in their lives. Likewise 49.7 per cent of Danes, 46.5 per cent of

Britons and 44.7 per cent of Belgians think it would be a "good thing".

By comparison - and confirming the relative satisfaction of the Dutch evident from my own findings - only 35.5 per cent of respondents in the Netherlands think it would be a "good thing" whereas 41.2 per cent think it would be a "bad thing".

"Close down and start again"

The so-called United Kingdom suffers, unsurprisingly, from a particularly acute case of 'terminal alienation', with only half of under 25-year-olds voting in the 1992 British general election, compared with about 77 per cent of the adult population.

Evidence of disillusionment with politics comes from two in-depth sociological studies. The first, undertaken by the Socioconsult subsidiary of MORI in 1994, found that 45 per cent of British men and 55 per cent of women in the 18-34 age group agreed with the statement "I'm not interested in politics". The figures for the 15-17 age group were 52 per cent and 68 per cent respectively.

In response to the statement "it will always be impossible to reform the system enough - we need to close most of it down and start again", 35 per cent of men and 40 per cent of women agreed. The younger age group agreed by 48 per cent and 47 per cent respectively.

Another statement ran "I feel more and more remote from the big political institutions". No less than 80 per cent of male respondents in the 18-34 age group agreed with this and 75 per cent of women (also 66 per cent of males and 71 per cent of females in the 15-17 age group). It is noticeable however that, in this case, the percentages for the 35-year-olds and above were even higher!

Socioconsult also identified a social milieu which the company dubbed 'the underwolf', meaning people who would traditionally be classed as underdogs but, though alienated, resist or 'bite back' rather than accepting things passively.

Members of this milieu agree with the statements "if I had a chance I would emigrate" [49 per cent of respondents to a 'Daily Telegraph' opinion poll in 1993 said they would prefer to live abroad if they could] and "I do not feel that I'm part of the British system, and I'm proud of it"!

The Socioconsult report states that over half of the 18-24 groups are attached to the 'underwolf' value to a greater or lesser degree and concludes: "It is less that these people feel they have moved apart from society; it is rather that society has moved apart from them".

In the light of the above no one should be surprised at the findings of another MORI poll on British teenager aspirations. Conducted on behalf of the City and Guilds institute in 1995 this study, which comprised interviews with some 1200 youngsters aged 15-18, found that one out of six respondents thought the thing they would least like to do is become a Member of Parliament. The last job anyone wanted among the options presented was that of the Opposition leader, Tony Blair.

The most searching recent examination of the attitudes of British youth toward their leaders is contained in the report 'Freedom's Children: Work, relationships and politics for 18-34 year olds in Britain today'. Published in 1995 by the Demos think-tank, in association with the Rowntree Trust, the report is the culmination of a year-long study involving in-depth qualitative and quantitative research. One of the objectives of the study was to investigate how to "create a sense of common purpose and ownership in the political system".

In its summary the report concludes that "for this generation [nb the 18-34 year olds] politics has become a dirty word" and then adds that "similar trends of disconnection are apparent in other countries, where they have prompted a far more serious response than in the UK." So some politicians, it seems, are taking note!

The report's authors go on to say that "there are strong signs of discontent: deep-seated distrust of the system, and frustrated ambitions, particularly amongst women." In the words of a 23-year old Scottish university graduate: "We have seen that nothing rigid will last and that any ideal put into the hands of a government will be perverted to its own interests."

These sentiments reflect not only the ineffectuality of government in dealing with social aspirations, but also the lack of opportunity and recognition in the private sector which, in turn, ultimately means ineffectual government.

The Demos study finds that people under 25 are four times less likely to be registered as voters than any other age group, less likely to vote for or join a political party, and less likely to be politically active. Only 6 per cent of 15-34 year olds describe themselves as 'very interested in politics'. On the other hand, the study did find some evidence that younger generations have become more willing to protest, so there may be hope yet.

The Demos report concludes that "the overwhelming story emerging from our research, both quantitative and qualitative, is of an historic political disconnection. In effect, an entire generation has opted out of party politics... the shift away from tradition and the decline of deference really begins in the 35-55 year old age group, but is steadily deepening with younger age groups who are fast losing respect for, and even interest in, the people in charge".

Extrapolating their findings to other countries, the authors add: "Some attribute this solely to the peculiarities of the British parliamentary system, or to having one party in power for so long. But these patterns are not peculiar to Britain. There are parallels in almost every industrialised country. In Germany there is mounting concern about falling political participation: a recent survey found young people are 50 per cent less likely to join parties, and whilst there were was a 77.5 per cent turnout rate in the 1990 Bundestag elections, amongst people aged 18-25 the rate dropped to just 62.5 per cent. France too has been exercised by youth alienation: former President Mitterand was so concerned that he commissioned a poll of the views of France's 15-25 year olds (and, ironically, proceeded to alienate them further by the manner in which the poll was carried out)."

All these studies detect, particularly in the under-25s, a retreat from social involvement into a personal, internalised world composed of partnership, family and friends. With the difficulties, real or imaginary, confronting them in the world outside, they are acting in a pragmatic, realistic, even slightly cynical way.

A study of these reports is enough to convince of the mindset of Europeans between the ages of 15 and 35. The absence of any inclination to revolt is as much a reflection of their commonsense as of a sense of futility.

These young people, in contrast to militant Baby Boomers, espouse values that are solid, supportive, even bourgeois. They tend to think that the stereotype of 'Generation X' is abusive.

They have an easy relationship with nature in an animist rather than in a cerebral, 'environmentalist' sense. They are motivated by the need for security, both emotional and financial, and cherish their relationships with the older generations.

With employment levels and uncertainty what they are now, how long will this last?

It would be wrong to think that these young Europeans do not feel involved with the big issues. Many of them are deeply concerned about things like global warning, traffic congestion and animal rights.

But they are equally convinced that the existing political structures are neither competent nor motivated to deal with these single issues in an effective way. Our political leaders need to restore confidence, to demonstrate that they are indeed capable of addressing the concerns of European youth.

But, with their credit so low, can they do this?

Corruption and ambiguous conduct

The apparent inability to solve the problems that most keenly affect the average European citizen - jobs, security, a stable currency - contrasts with aspects of government that are considered to be increasingly superfluous if not meddlesome.

An extreme example is the Tory government in the UK which, sensing its loss of public support, set out to win back ground through a bout of hyperactivity. This prompted 'The Economist' to say that "barely a week goes by without a new half-baked initiative". Government by gimmick.

But more importantly, the reputation of our political classes has been massively eroded in recent years by repetitive cases of corruption and ambiguous conduct. Such cases have been endemic in Italy, Greece, Austria, Spain, France and Britain, which specialises in a local variety known as 'sleaze'.

Reporting on the mood of young people in Spain in late-1995, 'The European' newspaper said that "the country needs to undergo a purification process whereby faith in public institutions is restored. Young Spaniards feel that if the government is corrupt, the entire state is corrupt. They are still committed to social causes but have become alienated from politics."

In the UK, a Gallup poll undertaken in June 1995 found that two-thirds of the British population thought that MPs made a lot of money by using public office improperly.

Abusive centralisation of power has, of course, made Britain something of a special case. But the concentration of power and privilege on a relatively small percentage of the people is a feature of all European democracies.

When you have - as in the case of Austria, Sweden, Finland and Ireland - a total population of less than ten million, it is hardly surprising that, when the really important issues are being discussed, almost everyone knows everyone else. It is said that even in the democratic Netherlands, with 15 million inhabitants, the major decisions are taken or at least directly influenced by an elite once known as 'the Mertens 200'.

Part, though not all, of the image problem faced by Europe's politicians reflects the time-honoured tradition that public office automatically provides both the responsibility and opportunity for extensive largesse in benefiting political friends and relatives. The principle is particularly though not exclusively entrenched in the countries of southern Europe.

Attitudes to corruption are themselves a reflection of the cultures concerned. Yves Meny, a French political scientist, makes the point that the very fact that bureaucracies in Latin countries are inefficient, due to the overstaffing and feather-bedding associated with a 'mamma state', encourages the emergence of 'fixers', *hommes de confiance*, and the like.

"People in the south are willing to accept corruption because they see it exists in everyday life and because everybody believes in the redemption of sin", he says. Papal indulgences, and all that. "In the north, the bureaucracy is more at the service of the common citizen than the state."

Maybe, but there are exceptions to this north-south rule. As a British sociologist pointed out to me, England (as opposed to Scotland or Wales) is a nominally Protestant country but its behaviour is decidedly Catholic: the Whitehall bureaucracy is definitely not at the service of the common citizen.

Italy's notorious system of *clientelismo* (what the 'Financial Times' called " a system of *cheques* and balances"!) or more specifically *lottizzazione* - the practice, inherited from Ancient Rome, of filling top public-sector and banking posts with political acolytes - is now happily under attack. Happily for us common citizens.

But little has yet been done to curb Spain's *enchufismo* ('plugging-in'), Austria's highly institutionalised *Proporz* (a Viennese version of Italy's *lottizzazione*) and Greece's *rousfeti* (the same thing) and mesa ('connections'). France hasn't needed to invent anything like this: it already has its *énarques,* the elite inner circle of graduates from the *Ecole Nationale d'Administration.*

High-level horsedealing

With public suspicions fuelled so heartily, it is not surprising that young people look at goings-on on the international scene with misgiving. The high-level horsedealing evident at climactic moments in European affairs are hardly calculated to restore public confidence in democracy.

Back in 1985 the American journalist Jane Kramer put her finger on the problem when she said that "the commitment to a European community grew out of the Second World War - out of a common experience of demented nationalism and the impulse, after that experience, to soften borders and create connections".

Yet, she continued, "the agreements that have been signed in Brussels since 1962 by politicians determined to promote the interests of France, say, or Germany or England while defending the rhetoric of 'Europe' have got so complicated by now, so elaborate, that it is much easier to add to them than to explain them, let alone make them work." Maastricht and the IGC came later...

The byzantine and often clandestine nature of Council of Minister dealings - now being energetically challenged by the new Nordic members of the European Union - have also contributed to the cynicism. On the other hand the system has served member governments well, enabling them to paper over some of their compromises for the benefit of public opinion back home.

But the image of member state governments has been further harmed by collective ditherings over such major foreign affairs issues as Bosnia and the recent Greek-Turkish dispute. In the words of Vaclav Havel, someone who understands the importance of personal convictions, Europe's leaders have displayed "a mentality marked by caution, hesitation, delayed decision-making and a tendency to look for the most convenient solutions", in fact all the things that are guaranteed to alienate European youth.

Strictly domestic discontent with government has often been deflected at the Union institutions by the very people who have been making the decisions as members of the EU's Council of Ministers. While the cynicism inherent in this little trick may escape many young Europeans, it does nothing to enhance the reputation of national politicians with those who understand the mechanics of the European Union.

Another factor that contributes to the apathy of the young is the lack of emotive content in politics and the appeals of politicians. In addition to the breakdown of community life, the influence of TV, and discos, British political scientists and psephologists blame, in the words of 'The Economist', "the emergence of a new sort of politics, based on shopping for policies rather than tribal loyalties". But policies, even discos, seem preferable to tribal loyalties.

With a few exceptions concentrated at the right wing of the spectrum, today's politicians - increasingly enmeshed in a global society, yet often balancing uncomfortably on the faultlines between national politics and the new Europe - are, or at least behave like, 'technicians'. The emotional appeal that politics used to have is no longer evident, for better or for worse. There may also be the lurking suspicion that effective power has passed from the political classes to the private sector.

Western European countries, with a few marked exceptions, give the impression of no longer being caring societies. With Thatcherism and the Yuppie generation (happily superseded by these new generations), plus the euphemism of downsizing and so-called 'reengineering', the world has become a rather nasty place. The free-market economy is as vulnerable to hijacking by a business oligarchy - in the names of liberalisation, privatisation, self-regulation and all that is holy - as democracy is to hijacking by politicians.

But at least European nations look like retaining a vestige of their social security systems - not because the politicians are anxious to keep them, but because they are too cowardly to face the public outrage that would result from their abandonment.

Public opinion and the media in the free-market West have made a serious mistake in consigning all other dogma indiscriminately to the dustbin of history. That the emotive appeal they offer is still there is evident from recent events in the culturally more collectivist societies of central and eastern Europe. The West, meanwhile, is in a state of suspended animation.

From gap to vacuum

What started out as a credibility gap between the political establishments of the Union's member states and their publics is now developing into a generational void within European society and, ultimately, a dangerous vacuum.

Some countries, notably Italy, are making a conscious effort to clean up the mess. Inspired by the initiative of Judge (now Minister) Di Pietro, the judiciary in Italy, Spain, France, Belgium and the United Kingdom - not forgetting the European Court of Justice - have acquired the admirable, if not entirely constitutional, habit of blowing the whistle on the executive branch.

In the eyes of the public and also the minds of some judges - surprisingly now even the German courts - big business is caught up in the process and suspected of guilt by association.

Pent-up public disapproval can shame politicians into action. This happened for example when British MPs, after harrumphing over the injustices of a proposal to enforce statutory disclosure of consultancy earnings, caved in to public opinion and passed a parliamentary motion in favour.

Yet, despite these concessions to public outrage, there is not much evidence that the political classes are aware of the gravity of the situation. If they are, they are not doing much about it.

Failure to recognise the gulf that is developing between them and the young people of Europe will create the kind of situation adored by demagogues and political opportunists. There are a number of these around and - who knows? - the younger generations might throw up one or two of their own.

Yet their own political naivety stands in the way. When questioned by Britain's 'Harpers & Queen' magazine, one interviewee said: "In a few years, our age-group will be in power and we'll be able to change things." I wonder.

The other danger is the erosion of the nation-state's justification for demanding the loyalty of its citizens. Of course, with the decline in public standards we are witnessing, we may ask what virtue there is in loyalty in any case.

The nation-state is losing its legitimacy by default. As it was a largely artificial creation in the first place, any attempt to sustain it must be motivated by popular sentiment, or by despair at finding a viable alternative. Not a pretty prospect!

What is certain is that many young Europeans would like the establishment as it is to go away. But no one relinquishes power and privilege without reason.

The best reason of all would be a revolution, but the present generation appears not to share the militancy of the Generation of '68 - and even that revolution lived up to its name by going around, French-fashion, in circles. After throwing *pavés* at the gendarmes, the young people went home for dinner with *maman et papa* in Neuilly-sur-Seine.

In reality it is the people on the other side of the old Iron Curtain who have posed the only real challenge to the political establishment in recent times. I remember standing by the Berlin Wall one week after *Die Wende* and saying to no one in particular that it might have been a good idea if the movement had continued westwards.

While the jury may still be out on what constitutes the best workable political system, the public verdict everywhere seems to be that there are very few good politicians. Power corrupts...

Whatever Now?

"Most of the nations of Europe have evolved through a fusion of regional loyalties, and their reconciliation calls for the exercise of tolerance and must always be subject to reservations"

E Esteyn Evans, *'The Personality of Ireland'*

"There is nothing more difficult to plan or more uncertain of success or more dangerous to carry out than an attempt to introduce new institutions, because the introducer has as enemies all those who profit from the old institutions"

Niccolo Machiavelli, *'The Prince'*

"The plurality of cultures is irreducible"

Sir Isaiah Berlin

"It [Benelux] was so successful, in fact, it was admired and envied by other Europeans. The French envisaged the addition of their own country and Italy to Benelux, the result to be called Fritalux, an unfortunate name suggestive of fried potatoes (les frites) and an inexpensive soap curiously used by affluent movie stars (Lux)."

Luigi Barzini, *'The Europeans'*

"Sovereignty has long since become an empty shell"

German Christian Democrat (CDU) policy statement, 1995

"If nationalism we must have, and in some measure we must, let us plump for a modulated, liberal, embracive, self-conscious nationalism - debilitated but therapeutic, like the virus in a polio vaccine. Surely nationalism red in tooth and claw is not the only kind"

Henry Louis Gates, Harvard University

"Like the natural world, the world of geopolitics does not easily change its species"

'The Economist', 5/1/1996

"Why should we found a new state in the new Europe? The states will wither away"

Xabier Arzallus, leader of the Basque Nationalist Party

It seems that, echoing the words of E Esteyn Evans, much of the tolerance has gone and the reservations are greater than ever. Cleaning up the Augean stables will not be enough to remotivate disaffected European youth.

Having presented its survey findings, the Demos report quoted in the previous chapter gave its conclusions: "The first step is to reconnect politics: to make it more accessible and more meaningful so as to restore trust. The potentially explosive alienation we have uncovered requires a totally different approach to politics - new styles of leadership, new languages, and new mechanisms. We know that young people want more honest and open styles of leadership; ones that fit their attachment to authenticity. We know that the problem of trust can only be addressed by governments delivering on their promises. But what could be done in terms of policy to re-engage commitment?"

What indeed? The Demos authors offer a range of suggestions relating to the techniques of consultation: referenda, voter juries, new voting techniques, Parliamentary debates on Internet, and so on. Yet is it not possible that the alienation of young people reflects the fundamental irrelevance of our macropolitical arrangements to the world we now live in?

If disenchantment is causing people to take their distance from the centres of power, the need for identity and in some cases a sense of nostalgia is prompting them to rediscover their roots. In the words of a Scots ethnologist, Ross Noble, "Europe never was peopled solely by the dominant ethnic and cultural groupings, and at the end of the 20th century, it is even less homogeneous than in the past. The fruits of imperialism and the slow and painful emergence of a one-world economy have added to the proliferation of minority groups which have always been a significant element in the make-up of Europe's population."

The idea of a Europe of the Regions has been around for a long time. As far as I can tell - and I suspect there's more to it than that - the concept was first aired by the Englishman Richard Cobden and the Frenchman Victor Hugo. Later it was taken up by an Austrian count, Richard Coudenhove-Kalergi, and by yet another Austrian, Leopold Kohr, who published an essay in 1941 entitled "Disunion Now: A plea for a Society Based Upon Small Autonomous Units". He argued that Switzerland had thrived not because of a national sense of identity but because of the smallness of its administrative units, the cantons.

In more recent times, the concept has been espoused by Richard Mayne, Professor Northcote Parkinson of 'Parkinson's Law' fame, and a musician-journalist, Mike Zwerin, who wrote a book entitled "A Case for the Balkanisation of Practically Everyone". Balkanisation? Well, er...

In one of a number of papers on the subject, Professor Parkinson identified what he then saw - and what many of us would still see today - as efficient nation-states, for example Finland and Denmark. He noted that these were "of merely provincial size with populations of about four to seven million" and went on to say that, "where the population exceeds ten million, there is a manifest case for decentralisation".

Most recently the case has been taken up by a Dutchman, one of the Heinekens of beer fame (it seems that, in this area of politics, everyone gets involved!). With the help of researchers at Leiden University he took up the ideas propounded by Northcote Parkinson and pleads for a redefinition of Europe that both respects cultural distinctions and limits administrative areas to no more than ten million people.

In his introduction to 'The United States of Europe (A Eurotopia?)' A H Heineken says: "Let us in this context not forget that our present nations are also artificial and, in many

142

cases, quite recent inventions. Government and cultural elites may have made us think otherwise, but let us remember that their line of thinking is embedded in (accepted) chauvinistic nationalism".

Further on, the Heineken document states: "The nation-states are quite often inventions of intellectual elites, propagated on the people concerned through education and the media. During this process traditions and 'national heritages' are created."

These eminent Europeans have kept on coming back to the same essential idea. It was also taken up by an American, Strobe Talbott, in a commentary in 'Time' newsmagazine, where he talked about "a devolution of power not only upward toward supranational bodies and outward toward common-wealths and common markets but also downward toward freer, more autonomous units of administration that permit distinct societies to preserve their cultural identities and govern themselves as much as possible. That American buzz-word empowerment - and the European one subsidiarity - is being defined locally, regionally and globally all at the same time."

Ah, subsidiarity! You will find it in the preamble to the Maastricht Treaty, which says that the signatories are "resolved to continue the process of creating an ever closer union among the peoples of Europe, in which decisions are taken as closely as possible to the citizen in accordance with the principle of subsidiarity".

Yes, but when European politicians talk about subsidiarity, they only mean subsidiarity as far as it suits them... and no further. Indeed the Treaty of Rome never mentioned 'regions', but we have come a long way since.

As Jordi Pujol, President of the Generalitat of Catalonia, pointed out in a speech to the European Union's Committee of the Regions in 1994: "There is a great danger that the

The World was already Global

"... there must be a natural political map of the world which gives the best possible geographical divisions for human administrations. Any other political division of the world than this natural political map will necessarily be a misfit, and must produce stresses of hostility and insurrection tending to shift boundaries in the direction indicated by the natural political map.

These would seem to be self-evident propositions were it not that the diplomatists at Vienna neither believed nor understood anything of the sort, and thought themselves as free to carve up the world as one is free to carve up such a boneless structure as a cheese. Most of the upheavals and conflicts that began in Europe as the world recovered from the exhaustion of the Napoleonic wars were quite obviously attempts of the ordinary common men to get rid of governments that were such misfits as to be in many cases intolerable...

The essential idea of nineteenth-century nationalism was the 'legitimate claim' of every nation to complete sovereignty, the claim of every nation to manage all its affairs within its own territory, regardless of any other nation. The flaw in this idea is that the affairs and interests of every modern community extend to the uttermost parts of the earth."

H G Wells, *'The Outline of History'* (1940)

principle of subsidiarity will be applied only to the relation between the states and the European Commission and not to the sub-state entities".

Charles Handy elaborated the decentralisation theme in 'The Empty Raincoat': "If we want to reconcile our humanity with our economics, we have to find a way to give more influence to what is personal and local, so that we can each feel that we have a chance to make a difference, that we matter, along with those around us. We have no hope of charting a way through these paradoxes unless we feel able to take some personal responsibility for events. A formal democracy will not be enough."

"We have to find another way", Handy continues, "by changing the structure of our institutions to give more power to the small and to the local. We have to do that, with all the untidiness which it entails, while still looking for efficiency, and the benefits of co-ordination and control. More is needed, therefore, than good intentions to 'empower' the individual to do what we want him or her to do. The structures and the systems have to change, to reflect a new balance of power. That means federalism."

Handy's words strengthen the belief that Europe's future also lies in generating grassroots industry - activities which develop literally from the ground up and knit together the fabric of local communities with a sense of common purpose. Italy offered a telling example in the 1995 national elections when 42 per cent of the vote in the Treviso area went to the Lega Nord.

This northern Italian community boasts 56,000 small firms, one for every eight families in the region, which together accounted for over $7.5 billion of exports in 1995 - almost as much, according to 'The Economist', as the whole of Greece "and the same as the southern Italian regions of Sicily, Apulia, Campagna and Calabria put together".

None other than Eric Hobsbawm concedes that a Europe of the Regions, though he doesn't use the phrase, has some merit: "... small states are today economically no less viable than larger states, given the decline of the 'national economy' before the transnational one. It may also be argued that 'regions' constitute more rational sub-units of large economic entities like the European Community than the historic states which are its official members."

In the conclusion to his book, Hobsbawm talks of "a world which can no longer be contained within the limits of 'nations' and 'nation-states' as these used to be defined, either politically, or economically, or culturally, or even linguistically. It will be largely supranational and infranational, but even infranationality, whether or not it dresses itself up in the costume of some mini-nationalism, will reflect the decline of the nation-state as an operational entity."

Shifting sovereignty

A Europe of the Regions would not only inhibit the kind of nonsense that now goes on in national and, to some extent, international politics. It would also bring the map of Europe back into line with reality. Of course, the interpretation of reality has to be economic as well as cultural. In terms of trade, Kortrijk falls as much within the economic orbit of northern France as it does within Belgian Flanders, just as northern Alsace falls within the job-creating orbit of the Saarland. In such cases, economics triumphs over history.

The European Union has its own Committee of the Regions, but it is difficult to qualify this as much more than a talking shop of 222 people. According to a Eurobarometer survey conducted in 1995 across the Union's member states, 70 per cent of those interviewed had never even heard of the Committee. They should have done, if only because it made a public ass of itself at the outset by trying to manipulate the recruitment process and create 'jobs for the boys' in the best traditions of *lottizazzione, enchufismo, Proporz, mesa,* etc.

A majority in the EU's Reflection Group, set up to examine issues prior to the Intergovernmental Conference (IGC), supported the idea of giving the Committee the status and rights of a full European institution. But it is hard to imagine Europe's present leaders enthusiastically promoting a process which would shift sovereignty from nations to regions. The most they have been been prepared to do is buy off the more obstreperous - first the German *Länder*, now the Catalans and the Belgian communities - by arranging occasional and largely symbolic representation on the Council of Ministers.

In short, none of the national political classes has done anything to transfer major powers to any body other than the European Union's own institutions and, most importantly, the Council of Ministers itself - where, unless the Member States accept the principle of qualified majority voting, the most reluctant will still have control of their destinies, albeit in a roundabout way.

They are certainly not prepared to cede any real authority to the European Parliament, as was evidenced by the shabby treatment doled out on the occasion of the IGC review of Maastricht. As Pauline Green, leader of the Socialist MEPs, said at the time: "It beggars belief that EU countries can contemplate reforming the treaty to make the EU more open and accountable and at the same time exclude the only directly elected Union institution."

Yes, but do member state governments - pace the Nordic countries - have any genuine intention of making the EU more 'open and accountable'? A Europe of the Regions would certainly encourage greater transparency. With less likelihood of conflicting internal interests, administrations

147

would have less to dissemble, less to hide, as well as greater difficulty in hiding it.

Two other positive consequences would apply at the level of public opinion. First, a restored sense of the democratic legitimacy of government. Secondly, and more arguable in terms of its external implications, an enhanced sense of social solidarity at regional level.

In fact some member states have moved a short way down the road towards regionalisation, as described in chapter 7. In many cases the impetus comes from below: as Charles Richards says in his book 'The New Italians', "the vision of a Europe of the regions is enormously appealing to Italians".

It also appeals to others. A Eurobarometer survey conducted among some 15,800 people in the Union's member states in 1995 found that, despite the continuing process of enlargement of the European Union, the concept of 'region' had lost none of its force and that the degree of identification with a region was still very high - although, it has to be added, this phenomenon was more developed in the old than in the young.

While 90 per cent of respondents identify with an area smaller than the country they belong to (the Greeks, Danes, Irish and Portuguese show the greatest attachment to their countries), the definition of 'region' varies from country to country. In twelve of the 15 member states - and notably again Greece, Denmark and Ireland, plus Finland, - people tend to identify with their town or village. In some other countries - most markedly Spain but, to a lesser extent, France - it is the region, 'autonomous' or otherwise, that counts.

The strongest regional attachments, regardless of what is meant by 'region', are to be found in Greece, Portugal and Austria (the Greeks seem to identify with everything - village, market town, region, country!). It is interesting to note that the Eurobarometer study found that Belgians, of both communities, were the Europeans who had developed their regional or local attachments the most since the previous study in 1992.

A Pandora's box of self-interest

As with all radical ideas, there are a number of problems with the concept of a Europe of the Regions - at least four of them.

The first is quite obviously the awful problem of persuading the present political elites to foresake their powers and privileges, even if there were room for them in the new order of things - something that European youth seems to think is not the case.

Historically, nation-state governments have harboured a wariness toward the intentions of their administrative underclasses. In the words of Jordi Pujol, the Catalan president, "it would be fruitless to ignore the distrust and suspicion with regard to the Regions which continues to exist at the level of the State and at the level of important sectors of the European political classes". He maintains that the nation-states have always been unitarist, centralist, even Jacobin in outlook. Jacobinism first emerged in France, but it subsequently left its mark on Italy, Spain, even Portugal.

Changing the order of things also goes against the grain of human nature. To quote Fernand Braudel, the French historian, people's sense of nationhood draws on "a thousand touchstones, beliefs, ways of speech, excuses, in an unbounded subconscious, in the flowing together of many obscure currents, in a shared ideology, shared myths, shared fantasies". Unfortunately the myths and fantasies often take over.

The second problem is that the headache and expense of maintaining and ultimately integrating the administrative functions of the individual components of a Europe of the Regions would be multiplied by the number of entities involved: from the current 36 European sovereign states (some of them less sovereign than others), excluding the CIS countries, to a total of maybe 80 regions.

As Belgium has already found out to its cost, regionalising what was national tends to result in increased layers of bureaucracy and higher taxes. And the German federal government estimates that the amalgamation of Berlin and Brandenburg would have produced an administrative saving of at least one billion DM if it had gone through.

A third problem is the act of defining what constitutes a region in the sense implied, i.e. a coherent community economically, culturally and possibly linguistically. It should be remembered, particularly in the light of recent events, that the reorganisation of southeastern Europe on the collapse of the Austro-Hungarian Empire was dictated by the Wilsonian doctrine of drawing the new frontiers along 'national' lines (see page 14).

Recent events have confirmed that this well-meaning if muddled effort to respect apparent realities - something that has been described elsewhere as a "high-minded and wholly mischievous attempt to rewrite all of Eastern Europe's borders" - was destined to end in disaster.

The final problem - maybe one should say the ultimate dilemma - with the concept of a Europe of the Regions is the danger of harnessing regions to an exclusive cultural or linguistic identity and thereby creating a series of ghettos. It seems to make perfect sense at first sight but, since any kind of dotted line - whether it defines a nation-state or a region - is a pretty arbitrary thing, there is always a risk of its harming any minority interests within the area it circumscribes, particularly if this instrument gets into the wrong hands. It can also ultimately have a debilitating effect on society: In the words of a 11th-century Hungarian cleric, "a kingdom of one race and custom is weak and fragile."

A redistribution of dotted lines to respect linguistic and cultural realities can also open a Pandora's box of self-interest. Some regions, through geography or historical change, are likely to be disadvantaged, others favoured. Self-administration is no excuse for selfishness. If wealthy regions should fail to respect the EU's underlying principle of creating a level playing field, then the Union should be entitled to enforce solidarity levies and sanctions.

Experience in Belgium has shown that regionalisation has solved one set of problems only to create others. In the matter of inter-regional relations, the current 'haves', the Flemish, feel disinclined to offer any kind of charity or sympathy to the 'have-nots', the Walloons. This kind of attitude could have even more serious consequences in relations between the majority *within* a region and any cultural, linguistic and foreseeably ethnic minorities with which they might be expected to cohabit.

Other countries are sharing the Belgian experience of a selfish free-for-all. Speaking of the so-called autonomous communities in his own country, the Spanish philosopher Fernando Savater says: "They want the maximum benefits, without realising that there are other regions with fewer advantages". This view is echoed by the the president of the Andalusian regional administration, who concedes that the regions extract as much as they can from central government without taking into account the needs of the other communities.

The only sensible view, balancing the urge for identity against the need for consensus for the common good, has been beautifully expressed by Scots author Joyce McMillan. Writing in 'The European', she says that "one of the key political arts of the coming age... is the art of maintaining a strong and evolving national identity, as a civil society and as a culture, while recognising that political sovereignty is a commodity that cannot be absolute, often has to be shared, and is not the sine qua non of meaningful cultural survival."

The only acceptable solution for Europe is to develop a multi-ethnic - more exactly a multi-cultural - society with no dotted lines and no ghettos. That is the direction the European Union professes to go: in this context, a Europe of the Regions may look like a step backwards. But it is a step forward in the sense of breaking Europe out of the national-political constraints and misdemeanours it is currently burdened with.

The ultimate message has to be that, while respecting cultural entities, the creation of a Europe of the Regions also implies respect for individual human rights. The search for identity should not be allowed to override the claims of citizenship of those who do not happen to belong to the culture concerned. Otherwise, we will end up running head on again into issues of language and ethnic purity and will be back where we started - with a Europe of the Ghettos.

US President James Madison clearly expressed, two centuries ago, the case for eschewing political systems based on too narrow self-interest: "Extend the sphere and you take in a greater variety of parties and interests; you will make it less probable that a majority of the whole will have a common motive to invade the rights of the other citizens; or if such a common motive exists, it will be more difficult for all who feel it to discover their strengths and to act in unison with each other".

A uniform disenchantment

Talking of political systems, there are many other issues of a more technical nature which should be rightly left to the political scientists, of whom there are a great number and whose ranks I have absolutely no intention of joining.

I will limit myself to saying that proportional representation doesn't seem to have helped the Italians, just as the 'first past the post' system doesn't seem to have helped the British.

Not even direct democracy *à la suisse* is a notable success, with less than half the electorate voting in the National Council elections and only 35 per cent on average participating in referenda.

Referenda are, as described to me by Sweden's leading constitutional expert, "a brutal kind of decision-making". There are people as wise as, or wiser than, the rest of us to whom we should entrust the business of managing our affairs. The trouble is that, at the moment, we don't have the right people or, perhaps more importantly, the mechanisms of politics and government don't allow us to get the best out of the ones we have.

Maybe the younger and more alert people in politics - there are some! - will take matters into their own hands by abandoning ship. One remote possibility is a spontaneous migration of the better talent towards the European Parliament. There are already signs that something of the kind is happening in the ranks of Britain's Tory Party.

There is no obvious solution to our current dilemma. A leader in 'The Economist' of October 14 1995 concluded: "Look around the democratic world and you see a great variety of constitutional arrangements and a uniform disenchantment with politics. This cautions against expecting too much of constitutional reform."

But there are obviously some key challenges that, sooner or later, have to be faced. First, a selective clean-up of our national political establishments - already underway in some countries - and a redrawing of the most unrealistic dotted lines on the map of Europe. Then, a programme to encourage young people to involve themselves again in the future of their countries and of the European Union.

Even if we were left with the status quo, we could still do a better job of it. Ultimately, and no doubt greatly oversimplified, it comes down to this. Learning to live with other cultures (which also implies communities and countries) is like learning to live with other people. Cultures are different in the same way that individuals are different, it's a question of scale. If we can learn to live with our real neighbours, then we can learn to live with our national neighbours. It's all part of the process of growing up. Isn't it time we grew up?

We should also, in the process, give up the frantic search for that will-o'-the-wisp, a European identity. I have spent many hours puzzling fruitlessly to identify things, old or new, that are unique to Europe and at the same time common to all its cultures. I end up with a list of none.

Yet something in addition to proximity and wishful thinking gives us a sense of common interest and common purpose. I think it has been beautifully and conclusively summed up in a phrase of the French historian, Jean-Baptiste Duroselle: "No region in Europe can be fully understood in isolation from the rest."

If we dwell on the differences, then we have to concede that these differences are extraordinarily complementary. Moreover, every European culture contains the seeds of good and evil.

Rather than indulging in a desperate effort to harmonise, Europe's leaders would do better to mobilise interculturally the good impulses of each society, and checkmate interculturally the bad ones. This would release enormous creative forces. But our leaders would have to agree first on their individual perceptions of 'good' and 'bad' - a tough task since the differences between cultures are largely a matter of value judgements.

In reality Europe's politicians will probably fail to face up to these issues, or will fudge them, so that we end up in the new millenium with no greater sense of direction than today.

Consider the scenario set by Hamish McRae in his book, 'The World in 2020': "As far as Europe is concerned, a thousand years of history suggest that it will never become a single national entity. And so European integration will reach a point from which it cannot advance further, for the pull of nationalism is too strong. Within Europe, countries with a relatively stable past (like England) will retain such stability, while those with a more turbulent history (like Italy) will continue to have periods of turmoil. Regionalism will grow as smaller states and regions seek to assert their identities. If, from an economic point of view, Europe has to encourage integration - attacking its high costs, its commercial rigidities and getting better value from its social spending - then from a political point of view it has to appreciate the natural limits to integration."

For my part, I think we could be headed for a macropolitical meltdown. The politically informed would evoke the last days of the Austro-Hungarian Empire when, quite obviously, the structures no longer suited the reality.

Yet in fairness to the Austro-Hungarian Empire, which has been unduly vilified in more recent times, it outlived its validity but not some of its ideals. It had actively promoted multi-cultural society in regions as far apart as Vojvodina, in what is still called Yugoslavia, and Chernivitsi (Chernowitz) in Ukraine.

Today's national politicians are showing far less awareness of what it is to be European than Josef II or even Maria-Theresia did more than two hundred years ago!

"This is a transition period for the concept of patriotism. It is now the duty of every citizen to see that his or her country isn't wrong, or if it is, to react accordingly. Floods of refugees or acts of civil disobedience are the modern methods of dissent.

The partisans of that older form of devotion to an abstract cause regard their sentiments as pristine, as though endowed with a kind of vulnerable virginity. They tend to defend this virginity even when it is under no discernable form of attack. The recognisable symptoms of this reaction in people is an outraged solemnity, as though blasphemies, as yet unspoken, were trembling on subversive lips. (...)

But what is this virginity that is so irrestible to the iconoclast? Surely not the purity of race, that piece of Nazi absurdity dramatised by scantily dressed women of impressive proportions gambolling with disci? It is too late for all that. All that can be hallowed now is the irreversible mongrelisation of all races.

The British way of life, for instance, is a judicious mixture of Ancient British, Roman, Saxon, Danish and Norman ways of doing things, flavoured by many incidental condiments on the side. The magnificent language, far from being a flaunting of natural purity, is evidence of massive interference and borrowings, which have tempered the pliant blade of self-expression into the wonderful means of communication that it is.

The virginity, then, is the illusion. All nations, even in their essence, are amalgams, the result of a primeval jostling of tribes for better bits of territory, for water, for forests, for high places. The patriotic gleam in the eye is the result of an abstract concept, the fulfilling of some sort of human need by fantasy and make-believe."

Peter Ustinov, *'The European'*

Postscript

"Educated side by side, untroubled from infancy by divisive prejudices, acquainted with all that is great and good in the different cultures, it will be borne in upon them as they mature that they belong together. Without ceasing to look to their lands with love and pride, they will become in mind Europeans, schooled and ready to complete the work of their fathers before them, to bring to being a united and thriving Europe"

Dedication, European School, Brussels

"National parliaments in Europe's larger countries, which are themselves federations of tribal regions, know that they are likely to be squeezed out if and when Europe becomes a fuller federation. Understandably, they do not relish the thought."

Charles Handy, 'The Empty Raincoat'

"Why are parents going to the trouble of having children? Is it just to have them silently endorse the world's present mismanagement for yet another generation?"

Letter to 'The European'

"The Europe of the States doesn't work any more"

Antonis Tritsis, Mayor of Athens

"Wer nicht weiss woher er kommt, weiss nicht wohin er geht, weiss daher nicht wo er steht" [*"Anyone who doesn't know where he's coming from and doesn't know where he's going to, doesn't know where he is"*]

Otto von Habsburg

"I'll bet that within the next hundred years... nationhood as we know it will be obsolete"

Strobe Talbott, 'Time'

"The happiest women, like the happiest nations, have no history"

George Eliot

"I love my country too much to be a nationalist"

Albert Camus

158

The first quotation on the facing page sums it up. It's just a pity that the founding fathers of the European School forgot to mention the mothers who, besides bringing young Europeans into the world, have as important a part to play in the future of Europe as the fathers.

Male chauvinism apart, it seems to me and many others that European society is only scratching at the surface of its problems. Underneath, a crisis of monumental proportions is brewing. The choice of many young Europeans, those with the benefit of an advanced education and those without, to opt out of the political decision-making process is a symptom of something that goes even deeper: the absence of a vision for the future of European society.

The collapse of communism was no reason to believe that all was well in the world of the winners. Thatcherism and its consequences, including the yuppie generation, have torn into the fabric of a maybe old-fashioned morality which believed, among other things, in a proper balance between prospering together and profiting individually, between self-interest and solidarity.

If parents abandoned the big issues in the scramble to a service economy, children can be forgiven for their abandonment of politics. The surprising thing is that these young people are putting the simple human values of partnership, sharing and security back onto the map.

This is even more surprising when one considers the provocations that society is directing at these young people: not just mounting evidence of political corruption, incompetence and abuse, but also a dearth of employment opportunities and the prospect of having to support an aging population through the rest of life. What a package!

All of this makes it even more important to get European youth back into the mainstream of society. If now, maybe too late, we try to give them values that can be shared, will they recognise them for what they are?

If nothing else they should inherit the legacy of peoples who, for far too long, fought among themselves viciously and relentlessly, but ultimately learned to live with one another in tolerance.

The world has changed massively in the last fifty years, but western Europe still lives with the threat of social dislocation. Then, the problem was the divides that separated countries and cultures. 'Us' was the mother-country, 'Them' was the rest.

Now, the dislocation is within countries and cultures, the growing gulf between Europe's young people and the society they were born into. Today 'Us' is Europe's youth and 'Them' is the rest of us.

We have distanced ourselves from our history as warring nations, only to discover that the fight has been brought into our own backyards. This time, it will be difficult for us to demonise our opponents in the way we did in the past.

BIBLIOGRAPHY

Bartlett, Robert. *The Making of Europe*. London: Allen Lane, 1993.

Barzini, Luigi. *The Europeans*. London: Penguin, 1984.

Broome, Benjamin. *Exploring the Greek Mosaic*. Yarmouth, Maine: Intercultural Press, 1996.

Chabot, Jean-Luc. *Le Nationalisme*. Paris: Presses Universitaires de France, 1986

Couloubaritsis, Lambros; De Leeuw, Marc; Noël, Emile; Sterckx, Claude. *The Origins of European Identity*. Brussels; European Interuniversity Press, 1993.

Del Marmol, Catherine. *Ich ben belge*. Brussels: Editions La Longue Vue, 1994.

Denman, Roy. *Missed Chances*. London: Cassell, 1996.

Duroselle, Jean-Baptiste. *Europe: A History of its Peoples*. London: Viking, 1990.

Evans, E Esteyn. *Irish Heritage*. Dundalk, 1942.

Evans, E Esteyn. *The Personality of Ireland*. Dublin: Lilliput, 1992.

Gage, Nicholas. *Hellas: a Portrait of Greece*. Anixi: Efstathiadis, 1995.

Gellner, Ernest. *Nations and Nationalism*. Oxford: Blackwell, 1983.

Greenfeld, Liah. *Nationalism: Five Roads to Modernity*. Harvard University, 1992.

Handy, Charles. *The Empty Raincoat*. London: Hutchinson, 1994.

Heineken, A H. *The United States of Europe.* Amsterdam: Stichting voor de Historische Wetenschap, 1992.

Hill, Richard. *We Europeans.* Brussels: Europublic, 1995.

Hobsbawm, E J. *Nations and Nationalism since 1780.* Cambridge: Canto, 1990.

Institut für Empirische Psychologie. *Wir sind OK!.* Cologne, Bund-Verlag, 1995.

Kaplan, Robert. *Balkan Ghosts.* New York: St. Martin's Press, 1993.

Kennedy, Paul. *The Rise and Fall of the Great Powers.* London: Fontana, 1989.

Kramer, Jane. *Europeans.* New York: Penguin, 1990.

Kristeva, Julia. *Nations Without Nationalism.* Columbia University Press, 1993.

Lessing, Doris. *Prisons We Choose to Live Inside.* London: Flamingo, 1994.

Lewis, Flora. *Europe - A Tapestry of Nations.* New York: Simon & Schuster, 1987.

McRae, Hamish. *The World in 2020.* London: HarperCollins, 1994.

Nora, Pierre. *Les Lieux de Mémoire.* Paris: Gallimard, 1993.

Pinker, Steven. *The Language Instinct.* London: Penguin, 1994.

Platt, Polly. *French or Foe.* London: Culture Crossings, 1994.

Reed, John. *The War in Eastern Europe.* New York: Charles Scribner, 1916.

Richards, Charles. *The New Italians*. London: Penguin, 1995.

Richmond, Yale. *From Da to Yes*. Yarmouth, Maine: Intercultural Press, 1995.

Wells, H G. *The Outline of History*. New York: Garden City/Doubleday, 1949.

West, Rebecca. *Black Lamb and Grey Falcon*. London: Macmillan, 1942.

Wilkinson, Helen and Mulgan, Geoff. *Freedom's Children*. London: Demos, 1995.

Europublications

WeEuropeans

Whatever doubts we may have about Maastricht, many of us hold fervently to the idea of a united Europe. And opinion polls among the young show a growing commitment to the European ideal.

This Europe is all about people – people who differ in their tastes and habits but share the same values and ideals. Understanding them, understanding one another, is a crucial step in the process of creating a Europe where unity cohabits with diversity.

Richard Hill talks about the people in this book. He starts by describing, then attacking, the stereotypes and moves on to a witty and skilful analysis of each of the European cultures.

He then enlarges his theme with a comparative analysis of value systems and lifestyles, how people communicate, relate to one another and do business. The final chapter examines recent events and offers thoughts on where we go from here.

"...a fascinating book. His dissection of each nationality produces some wonderful sociological insights."

The European

"Richard Hill starts from the obvious to discover the difficult and makes an impressive success of it."

Emanuele Gazzo, *Agence Europe*

"A delightful and very funny book. I'll buy it!"

Derek Jameson, *BBC Radio 2*

"I can warmly recommend a wonderful book by Richard Hill, 'WeEuropeans'." **Libby Purves,** *BA High Life*

"A delightful and very funny book. I'll buy it!"

Derek Jameson, BBC Radio 2

"One of the most interesting books I've ever looked at"

Patrick Middleton, *Riviera Radio*

"Das Buch 'Wir Europäer' des Engländers Richard Hill ist in Brüssel zum absoluten Bestseller avanciert. Mild ironisch analysiert er die Gewohnheiten der Euro-Völker, deckt Gemeinsamkeiten und Unterschiede auf, weist auf Stärken und Schwächen hin"

Birgit Svensson, *Wochenpost*

"Il fallait être Britannique pour oser le pari, il fallait avoir vécu longtemps à Bruxelles pour le réussir. C'est le cas de l'Anglais Richard Hill"

Violaine Muûls, *L'Evénement*

"'WeEuropeans' hoort verplichte lectuur te zijn voor elke deelnemer aan een Eurotop. Het zou de sfeer opvrolijken en de besluitvorming versnellen. De Europeanen, binnen en buiten de EG, zouden er wel bij varen. Om hen gaat het toch altijd, beweren de regeringsleiders onvermoeid"

Henk Aben, *Algemeen Dagblad*

"Wir Europäer: Zum Lachen!"

BZ am Sonntag

"Een onderhoudend boek, dat gezien de huidige ontwikkelingen binnen de Gemeenschap niet alleen actueel, maar ook leerzaam is"

Haye Thomas, *Haagsche Courant*

"I bästsäljaren 'We Europeans' finns vi redan med på ett hörn, som ett hyggligt men gammaldags folk med dörrar som öppnas utåt... 'We Europeans', en munter och innehållsrik bok som snabbt blivit populär bland EG-folket"

Dagens Nyheter, Sweden

"Hill mainitsee sivumennen myös, että suomalaiset juovat paljon. Tämäkin mielikuvaongelma jälleen kerran! Lukiessa eteenpäin käy ilmi, että hän tarkoittaa maidon kulutusta"

Turun Sanomat, Finland

167

EuroManagers & Martians
Richard Hill

The Business Cultures of Europe's Trading Nations

EuroManagers & Martians

Looking at them simply as people, when we see them in the streets of Paris or when we visit them *chez eux*, our fellow-Europeans come across as a pretty odd lot – a far cry from the Single Market, harmonisation and all those dreary things.

But how do they behave in business? Put a German, a Frenchman, a Spaniard, an Italian, a Swede and, of course, a Brit together around a negotiating table and what happens? Either nothing at all – they just don't know how to deal with one another – or a lot! It's then that you realise that, despite all the constraints of working within a business environment, life à *l'européenne* is still full of surprises.

The simple fact, of course, is that it would need a super-human to leave his cultural baggage behind him simply because he puts on his coat to go to the office. This book examines the business cultures of Europe's main trading nations and offers useful insights into differences in attitudes to time, hierarchy, protocol, negotiating styles, acceptance of management disciplines and multicultural teamwork.

With so much cultural diversity even in business, the author wonders how on earth we are going to develop the Euromanager we keep hearing about, the person who is going to save us from the Japanese, the Asian Tigers and others. Will this Euro-superman-ager ever exist?

"The book is written from an alien's point of view, and it presents both carefully researched and anecdotal evidence in an entertaining read... Carefully steering a course away from the stereotype path, Hill gives well-considered and practical advice on conducting Eurobusiness." **The European**

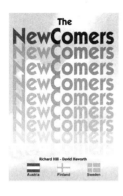

The
NewComers

'The NewComers'

a book that 'takes the lid off'
the Austrians, Finns and Swedes

Many months after Austria's, Finland's and Sweden's accession to the European Union, ignorance about these countries is as great as ever.

Maybe not where they are, or what they represent economically, but who they are, how they do business, what things are important to them and what are not.

Now Richard Hill and David Haworth, a public affairs consultant specialising in the Nordic countries, have collaborated to write **"The NewComers"**.

This book sets out 'to take the lid off' the Austrians, Finns and Swedes, and explain them to their fellow-Europeans and others. The Norwegians were also supposed to be included but, sadly, things didn't work out that way.

"The NewComers" presents a family portrait of each of the three countries - their virtues, their quirks, tastes, habits and sensitivities, together with relevant background on history and politics.

This book provides even the most mildly curious with a clear and entertaining introduction to those who, from now on, will have a growing influence on the nature of the "new EU".

"I would like to congratulate you on this publication, which is not only a delightful read, but gives at the same time a very comprehensive insight into these countries, their people and mentalities"
Austrian Embassy Official

"Your style is extremely lucid and filled with tolerance and humour. May I inscribe myself in the Richard Hill and David Haworth fan club?" **Swedish lawyer and lobbyist**

"Delightful! You seem to have got the essence of this extremely complex society" **British businesswoman in Vienna**

GREAT BRITAIN LITTLE ENGLAND

Britons have recently been bombarded and bludgeoned with books examining the reasons for their country's dramatic decline.

But, while offering heavily documented analyses of culprit 'constituencies' - labour, management, educators, civil servants, government itself - these books have stopped short of examining the mindsets, motivations and mannerisms common to the actors in the drama.

In this book, Richard Hill sets out to fill the gap. Starting with himself, he tries to get under the skin of the British - more specifically, the English - and understand where they go right and why they go wrong.

This is an entertaining and thought-provoking book by a Briton who has had the advantage of living outside his island culture, yet consorting closely with it, for the last 30 years.

"I found it fascinating reading. If I weren't British (sorry, English), I would have enjoyed it."

Stanley Crossick,
Belmont European Community Office

"Wonderful stuff. Witty and accurate without being cynical."
John Mole, author of 'Mind Your Manners'

"I am thoroughly enjoying reading it... it cheers up a Scottish Nationalist of a London evening!"

Margaret Ewing, MP

Have You Heard This One? An Anthology of European Jokes

Here are some of the better jokes we Europeans tell about one another. There are a lot of bad ones – far too many – but you will find none of them here.

Good European jokes are neither stupid nor abusive. They tell one something instructive about the way people from different cultures perceive one another. And some of these jokes shed light on the cultures of both the 'sender' and the 'receiver'.

Humour is the subtlest expression of culture, which explains why English people have difficulty in understanding German jokes. Even the psychology of humour is coloured by the attitudes of the different cultures. Yet there is common ground in European humour: some of these jokes turn up in various guises in various places.

As that eminent European Johann Wolfgang von Goethe said, rather severely: "There is nothing in which people more betray their character than in what they laugh at". Taken in the right spirit, humour is an excellent starting point for cross-cultural comprehension.

Us & Them						

Other books on European cultures are in preparation.

If you have difficulty in obtaining any of these books through your local bookstore, you can order from the publisher:

Europublic SA/NV,
Avenue Winston Churchill 11 (box 21), B-1180 Brussels, Belgium
Tel. +32-2-343.77.26 - Fax +32-2-343.93.30

Email: info@europublic.com
          europublic@msn.com
          100647.2266@compuserve.com

Websites: For detailed information on publications, please visit our
          website:
          URL INTERNET **http://www.understanding-europe.com**
          For information on Europublic's consultancy, training &
          speaking services:
          URL INTERNET **http://www.europublic.com**

Name: ....

Address: ....

....

....

Tel: .... Fax: ....

This book is about divides. About the dotted lines that arbitrarily separate people who have always had more in common than most of us would admit, about the gap that distances the younger generation from the older generations of Europeans, and about the gulf that is now widening between public opinion in Europe and its political classes - a gulf that is developing into a vacuum with serious, possibly lethal, implications.